The Book of
Leviticus

The Book of Leviticus

An Exposition by

Charles R. Erdman

BAKER BOOK HOUSE
Grand Rapids, Michigan 49506

Copyright 1951 by
Fleming H. Revell Company
Paperback edition issued 1982 by
Baker Book House
with permission of copyright owner

ISBN: 0-8010-3377-2

PHOTOLITHOPRINTED BY CUSHING - MALLOY, INC.
ANN ARBOR, MICHIGAN, UNITED STATES OF AMERICA

Worship the Lord
in the
Beauty of Holiness

Introduction

THE Book of Leviticus may be described as a directory for divine worship. The tabernacle had been erected at the foot of Mount Sinai. It was furnished with an altar of sacrifice, a laver, a golden "candlestick," a table of shew-bread, an altar of incense, and in the Holy of Holies above the mercy seat a glorious light was a symbol of the divine presence. How could a holy God be approached? What would be required of worshipers? What sacred seasons were appointed as special times of worship? The answers to these questions are found in this book.

The *Provision for Approach to God* included the offering of sacrifices on the part of worshipers and the mediation of priests in their behalf. The *sacrifices* were of differing forms, designed to express the need and the purpose of the worshiper. The "burnt offering" represented complete dedication of life. The "meat offering," or more correctly the "meal offering," symbolized service, as it consisted of vegetables which were the fruit of labor. The "peace offering" expressed fellowship. The "sin offering" was to secure expiation, and the "trespass offering" was made not only in confession of fault, but to give satisfaction for some invasion of the rights of others (Chs. 1-7).

The *priests* were the sons of Aaron, who served as high priest. They were ordained to their office by solemn rites and served in accordance with a prescribed ritual. They were all members of the tribe of Levi and were assisted in their tasks by other members of the same tribe. Thus the book was called "The Book of the Priests" or "The Book of the Levites," for it was designed as a manual to guide the priests and Levites in their sacred tasks (Chs. 8-10).

The *requisite for worship* may be summarized in one inclusive word, "holiness." This, indeed, is accepted as the key word of the book. It occurs more than eighty times. It is used of the divine purity and perfection of God Himself, but also is applied to whatever is set apart and dedicated to Him; thus the tabernacle and its furnishings and the offerings, as well as the priests and people, are declared to be holy. When so used it signifies separation, not only from sinful but also from common use, and describes both ceremonial and moral purity. In the central section of the book it refers to purification or cleansing. It describes how the unclean can be made clean (Chs. 11-15). This instruction reaches its climax in the ritual for the Great Day of Atonement, the central and supreme chapter of the book (Ch. 16). Moreover, moral purity, or holiness of life, is solemnly enjoined on all worshipers, people and priests alike (Chs. 17-22).

The *times for worship* composed a cycle of which the formative factor was the number seven. The seventh day was observed as the weekly Sabbath. Seven weeks after Passover, the first great feast of the year, came Pentecost, the Feast of Weeks. The seventh month was announced by the Feast of Trumpets; it included the Day of Atonement and the Feast of Tabernacles. The seventh year was observed as the Sabbatical Year of rest, and after seven sevens of years there was proclaimed the great Year of Jubilee. All these sacred feasts were signs and seals of consecration, and indicated that the worshipers, their time, their land, their persons, belonged to God (Chs. 23-26).

A concluding chapter dealing with the holiness of vows and tithes is added in the form of an appendix (Ch. 27).

However, the Book of Leviticus may be regarded not only as a "Directory for Worship" but as a *Code of Laws*. At Mount Sinai, according to divine directions, the tabernacle had been erected, but there an even more important event had taken place. A solemn covenant had been made between Jehovah and Israel. It was based on the so-called "Book of the Covenant," which contained the Ten Commandments and certain related laws. It specified that if Israel kept the covenant God would be their God and they would be His people, a "people for his own possession." Now that the covenant had been sealed solemnly with sprinkled blood, and now that the tabernacle had been dedicated, Jehovah, seated on His throne, gave through Moses to the children of Israel certain additional laws peculiar to Him as their God and to them as a nation of worshipers. Yet these laws related not only to worship but to all the activities and relations of life, to food and to rest, to cleanliness and purity, to marriage and divorce, to the rights of property, to the relation of rich and poor, and to all that would secure the physical, moral and spiritual well-being of the people. The exact regulations are not in force today, but they embody fundamental principles of civil law and national life. A nation cannot prosper which neglects to recognize the being and the will of God, or to make its legislation in conformity with His revealed will. Only by such recognition can a free people maintain liberty and justice and prosperity.

It is impressive to find a book of worship so immediately concerned with the practical conduct of life. There always has been a tendency to confuse ritual with religion, or to divorce forms of worship from morality and faith and purity of life. The people of Israel did not escape this peril. Later prophets found it necessary to rebuke a nation which was rendering service to God "with their lips" and with elaborate ceremonies, while their hearts were far from Him. The Book of Leviticus intimately connects the most exacting ritual with the demands of perfect holiness.

Furthermore, this is a *Treasury of Prophetic Symbols.* Herein lies its supreme value. This is a book of types and shadows which find fulfilment and substance in the redeeming work of Christ and in the lives of His followers. It was interpreted thus by our Lord and His apostles. He drew upon its symbols to interpret His atoning death, and the apostles found in Him the "Lamb of God," the divine Saviour who "bore our sins in his own body on the tree." The entire Epistle to the Hebrews is an interpretation of Leviticus. It finds in Christ the Great High Priest, who "put away sin by the sacrifice of himself," who "is able to save unto the uttermost those who come unto God by him."

Such a view at once removes the book from the sphere of mere antiquarian interest in which it would be regarded as only a discarded ritual of an ancient people. On the other hand, one needs to be warned against a temptation to give rein to unbridled fancy in studying the types of Leviticus. A safe rule is to limit the lessons we draw from Old Testament symbols to the teaching derived from such symbols by the writers of the New Testament.

In reading this book it may be well to keep in mind

three questions: (1) What did the exact provisions of the ritual signify to the ancient Israelites? (2) How is any specific type fulfilled by the person and work of Christ? (3) What application of the principle involved can be made to the life of a Christian? Even a partial answer to these questions will give to the book a practical and fascinating interest, and a more complete understanding will bring one to the very heart of the Christian Gospel.

C. R. E.

Contents

13

The Book of Leviticus

I

THE PROVISION FOR WORSHIP
LEVITICUS 1 to 10

SACRIFICE. [Chs. 1 to 7]

THE first words of Leviticus may be regarded as an index to its character or as an introduction to its contents. At least, they set forth its origin and its authority. "And the Lord called unto Moses and spake unto him out of the tabernacle of the congregation." It is true that this sentence is the preface to only the first section of the "Law of Sacrifice"; yet it is repeated in practically the same form fifty-six times in the twenty-seven chapters of Leviticus, and, therefore, may be taken as a declaration of the Mosaic origin and the divine authority of the entire book.

By what method God spoke to Moses it is useless to conjecture. We need not suppose that an audible voice issued from the mystery and glory of the Holy of Holies, nor that words were dictated which Moses reduced to writing. Nor need we deny that other men may have assisted Moses in his work, or may have composed or combined at a later date documents which embodied the statutes of the great lawgiver. It even may be conjectured that in the course of centuries these laws were edited or amended by men likewise inspired of God and qualified for their task. The only essential contention is this, namely, that it contains messages from God communicated through Moses as His agent.

To this fact our Saviour gave His specific witness. Whatever processes previously may have been involved in its production, the very Book of Leviticus which we have today is the book which was in the hands of our Lord. As to the Law of which it was a part, He declared this to be more abiding than "heaven and earth," and, further, that if the Jews had believed Moses they would have also believed Him (John 5:46, 47). Quite as definitely He endorsed the Mosaic source and inspired authority of Leviticus. When lepers had been healed He sent them to the priests because Moses had so commanded. This command is found only in Leviticus (Ch. 14:3-10). When defending His disciples for an alleged breach of Sabbath law, He refers to the authority of a statute found in this book alone (Ch. 24:9). He insists that the law of Leviticus in reference to the care of parents has the same divine authority as the Fifth Commandment (Matthew 14:3-6, Leviticus 20:9). When giving a summary of all the Commandments, He quotes from Leviticus, "Thou shalt love thy neighbor as thyself" (Ch. 19:18). The testimony of Christ is quite clear. The laws of Leviticus are the laws of Moses and were given by inspiration of God.

These statutes begin with the *Law of Sacrifice* (Chs. 1-7). Worship involves sacrifice. Indeed, among the Jews and other ancient peoples, sacrifices formed the essential feature of religious worship. One who approaches God must have something to offer. Such is the summons of the Psalmist:

Give unto the Lord the glory due unto his name:
Bring an offering and come into his courts. Psalm 96:8.

Our offering may be that of praise or prayer, of time or talents, or wealth or of life itself, but the surprising feature of our Christian worship is this: God Himself has provided for us a Sacrifice, even His own beloved Son. It is only in virtue of this sacrifice, only "in Christ," only as by faith we identify ourselves with Him, that our offerings are accepted and we have free access to God, receiving pardon and peace, and enjoying fellowship with Him.

The offerings prescribed for the Israelites were of various materials. They might be oxen or sheep or goats or even doves or pigeons. There also were certain accessories, such as flour or grain, salt, honey, frankincense, and wine. The animal sacrifices must be without blemish and of those regarded as ceremonially clean. They were domestic animals, closely associated with the worshiper, and representing his personal property. The exact offerings for each purpose and occasion were defined in the opening paragraphs of the Law of Sacrifice which contain *instructions for worshipers* (Chs. 1:1-6:7).

Also, the offerings were made in accordance with certain exacting forms, set forth in the next paragraphs of the law which embody the *ritual for priests* (Chs. 6:8-7:38). These forms included presentation of the offering "at the door of the tabernacle," placing the hands of the worshiper on the head of the offering, slaying of the offering, and the specified disposition of the flesh, the fat and the blood.

Why was God so pleased with these offerings that they could be called the "bread of God," or "food of God" (Ch. 21:6; 3:11)? Surely no intelligent Israelite entertained the gross idea, prevalent among heathen nations, that sacrifices were offered to supply the physical needs of a deity. It was understood more or less perfectly that God was a spirit and was pleased, not with the sacrifice, but with that which the offering of the sacrifice

symbolized, namely, gratitude, love, penitence, devotion
and trust. This is indicated in the prayers of the Psalmist:

The sacrifices of God are a broken spirit:
A broken and a contrite heart, O God, thou wilt not despise.
    Psalm 51:17.

I will offer to thee the sacrifice of thanksgiving,
And will call upon the name of the Lord. Psalm 116:17.

Let my prayer be set forth before thee as incense;
And the lifting up of my hands as the evening sacrifice.
    Psalm 141:2.

When not accompanied by reverence and faith, mere
forms of worship are never acceptable to God. Again and
again, the Hebrew prophets needed to rebuke the people
for presenting their offerings to God when their hearts
were far from Him. However, we are not to conclude that
when an Israelite did trust and love God, he needed to
make no offering to the Lord. These offerings were divinely ordained and carefully specified. Vain and empty
in themselves, they had deep significance when offered in
obedience and devotion.

As Christians we realize that these ancient offerings
are no longer demanded, since all they symbolized has
been fulfilled in the one perfect Offering, even in Christ,
who was wholly devoted and dedicated to God. Our faith
and love are expressed by accepting Him as our Sacrifice
and approaching God in His name. Thus we are not to
conclude that Christ is not needed if one seeks to be kind
and grateful and good. Rather we are to remember that
we are accepted as true worshipers when we express in our
lives our devotion to Him who is our Example and our
Lord. "Through him then," writes the apostle, "let us
offer up a sacrifice of praise to God continually," and "do

not forget to do good and to share what you have, for such sacrifices are pleasing to God" (Hebrews 13:15, 16).

Why, furthermore, did God ordain such a "repellant" ritual (Chs. 6:8-7:38)? Why the killing of these animals, why this shedding of innocent blood? It was designed to set forth the hideous character of sin. It was to emphasize the divine decree: "The soul that sinneth it shall die." It was to reveal the gracious provision whereby sinful man could approach a holy God and could receive pardon and enjoy fellowship with Him. This provision was by the acceptance of a life in place of a life. "The life . . . is in the blood" (Ch. 11:11). The blood which was shed was life poured out. The Hebrew worshiper was taught that the sacrifice was his substitute. His sin merited death, but the life which was offered secured forgiveness and atonement. The ancient worshiper learned that "without shedding of blood" there "is no remission of sin" (Hebrews 9:22).

The larger purpose of this perplexing ritual is seen when we regard its prophetic symbolism. There can be no doubt that it found its fulfilment in the atoning work of Christ. His herald announced His coming by the familiar significant words: "Behold the Lamb of God which taketh away the sin of the world" (John 1:29). He declared of His own mission that He had come "not to be ministered unto but to minister and to give his life a ransom for many" (Mark 10:45). When offering the wine at His memorial feast He declared, "This is my blood of the new covenant which is shed for many for the remission of sins" (Matthew 26:28). His disciple John also gave the assurance that "the blood of Jesus Christ . . . cleanseth from all sin" (I John 1:7); and he recorded his vision of the "great multitude" who had "washed their robes and made them white in the blood of the Lamb" (Revelation 7:14).

The offerings which symbolized the sacrificial work of Christ were divided into five classes known as "burnt," "meal," "peace," "sin," and "trespass." It is for us to discover what particular aspect of this work was typified by each of these offerings and what message is embodied for the followers of Christ. With this in view, it may be helpful to combine in a connected treatment what separately is recorded of each offering in the instruction for worshipers (Chs. 1:1-6:7), and in the ritual for the priests (Chs. 6:8-7:38).

THE BURNT OFFERING. [Chs. 1:1-17 and 6:8-13]

The first and most familiar of the sacrifices was the burnt offering, which expressed *dedication*. The very name indicates its distinct characteristic. The term means "that which ascends," that is, to Jehovah. The entire sacrifice was consumed by fire on the altar, so that it was also described as the "whole burnt offering." Of the other sacrifices, part was burned and part was eaten by the priests or even by the offerer himself; but of the burnt offering, all ascended to God in flame and smoke. Thus the Israelite was taught that entire consecration is essential to true worship. The offerings, from herds or flocks or fowls, were graded in value to correspond with the means of the worshipers, possibly indicating that even one who is most conscious of spiritual need may find access to God if coming in complete devotion and in the name of the true Sacrifice, our divine Lord.

The offering from the flock or herd must be ceremonially "clean," for that which could not be touched by man was not to be offered as a sacrifice to God. It also must be "without blemish," for God will not be pleased with worthless gifts but deserves the best we have.

"The Law of Sacrifice" provided that the worshiper must bring his offering in person. Others may lead us or aid us in worship, but none can worship for us. It might be noted, too, that this ideal act of worship was in public "at the door of the tabernacle of the congregation," that is, in the court near the brazen altar. Thus presenting the sacrifice indicated the desire for access to God and for divine acceptance. The worshiper was to "put his hand on the head of the burnt offering." This would express the surrender of the gift to God, and also the identification of the gift with the giver, and, further, the transfer to the sacrifice of all that the worshiper owed to God. This offering would "be accepted for him, to make atonement for him." "Atonement," literally "to cover," came to mean, as here, reconciliation and pardon. The sin of the offerer would be forgiven by the transfer of guilt to the sacrifice, which was regarded as his substitute.

Yet the dominant idea of this offering is not expiation but dedication. As the sacrifice is now killed and the blood sprinkled or poured on and about the altar, it is evident that the conception of atonement by blood is here present, but the picture of life given as an offering and the subsequent burning of the entire sacrifice indicate the supreme message of this offering, namely, complete consecration to God. The ascending of the sacrifice in flame and smoke, according to the divine direction, and the acceptance of it as "a sweet savour unto the Lord," were designed to show the self-dedication expected of every worshiper who seeks for access and acceptance in approaching God.

One further feature of this burnt offering is emphasized in the supplemental ritual appointed for the priests
(Ch. 6:8-13). Here it is provided that the fire once kindled on the brazen altar is never to be extinguished. It is
to be replenished, and a burnt offering is to be presented
for the people every morning and evening. Therefore, this
sacrifice came to be known as the "*continual burnt offering.*" The application is quite obvious. The consecration
which God requires of His people is not merely once for
all. It is to be continuous, yet renewed consciously at the
opening and the close of each day. "The fire shall be kept
on the altar continually; it shall not go out" (Ch. 6:9,
12, 13).

Such complete consecration as was symbolized by
this ancient institution of the burnt offering has been embodied and realized only in our Lord Jesus Christ. His
obedience was perfect. In Him was fulfilled the prediction of the Psalmist, "When he cometh into the world he
saith, Sacrifice and offering thou wouldest not, but a body
didst thou prepare for me. . . . Then said I, Lo, I am
come (in the roll of the book it is written of me) to do
thy will, O God" (Psalm 40:6-8; Heb. 13:5-7).

The first recorded words of our Lord were as follows:
"Wist ye not that I must be about my Father's business?"
(Luke 2:49). In His early ministry He said to His disciples, "My meat is to do the will of him that sent me and
to finish his work" (John 4:34). So He declared of His
latest teaching, "The Father hath given me a commandment, what I should say and what I should speak" (John
12:50). At last He could say to His Father, "I have finished the work thou gavest me to do." On the cross He
could repeat that word, "It is finished." He was "obedient unto death." He gave Himself "for us, an offering

and a sacrifice to God for a sweet smelling savour." As through His atoning death He secured our pardon, so in His perfect life He was our representative. He is our "Righteousness" and also our "Sanctification" (I Corinthians 1:30). He is at the same time our Sacrifice for sin and our Example for holy livng. If we are to be true worshipers we must yield ourselves with complete abandon to the will of God. Thus the apostle pleads with us, "I beseech you therefore, brethren, by the mercies of God, to present your bodies a living sacrifice, holy, acceptable to God, which is your reasonable service" (Romans 12:1). The apostle speaks here by way of both comparison and contrast. Our self-dedication as Christians is like the burnt offering. It consists of our "bodies" but also of our souls, our very selves, of which our bodies are the agents or instruments. These are "living" sacrifices, in contrast with the ancient offering the life of which was taken before the offering was placed on the altar. Like those sacrifices, our offering is "holy," or consecrated, as devoted to the service of God. It is "acceptable to God," like the burnt offering which was a "sweet savour" offering, well pleasing to God. It is "reasonable" or "spiritual," in contrast with material offerings. It is a "service" or a priestly ritual, for such consecration forms the most sublime of liturgies. The plea for such consecration is based on the "mercies of God." We yield ourselves to God, not that He may love us or grant us pardon and fellowship, but because He has loved us, and given His Son as the perfect Sacrifice. Because we have been "accepted in the beloved," "therefore" we yield ourselves to Him, and being filled and dominated by His Spirit, we "prove," or find out by personal experience, what the will of God is, that is, what in itself is "good," what is "acceptable" to God, what is morally "perfect" and complete.

THE MEAL OFFERING.
[Chs. 2:1-16 and 6:14-23, A.R.V.]

The meaning of a word changes in the course of time. Thus it is interesting, even amusing, to note that the "meat offering," as designated in the Authorized Version of the Bible, is the one offering which did not consist of "meat." It was the "meal offering," an offering of grain or cereals. It was made of fine flour. It might be presented in the form of cakes, which might be baked or fried or boiled. Or the offering could be of parched grain. When used for food, the meal was mixed with oil and salt, but neither leaven nor honey could be added.

The word in the original text which is translated "meal offering" means simply a "present." Thus the primary idea of this offering is that of a gift presented to God as an act of worship. Yet as this offering was the product of the soil, and the result of human labor, it symbolized the consecration to God of the fruit of one's labor. As this fruit was in the form of food, it indicated that all our toil or our activities should be dedicated to God, so that, as the apostle declares, "Whether ye eat or drink, or whatsoever ye do, do all to the glory of God" (I Corinthians 10:31). The ingredients included in the offering are significant. *Salt* was to be used as it would preserve from corruption. It was called "the salt of the covenant of thy God," for it would be a sign of the changeless covenant between God and His people.

Oil, which was used in preparing most forms of the "meal offering," was not only a usual constituent of daily food, it was a recognized symbol of the Holy Spirit. It points to the fact that persons who are dedicated to God can expect the power of His Spirit to guide and aid and empower them for all the experiences of daily life and service.

Incense was a symbol of prayer and of praise, so that as we offer to God the work of our hands, however humble our task, it is sanctified by continual petition and thanksgiving.

All *leaven* and *honey* must be excluded from that part of the offering which was burnt on the altar, for leaven was a symbol of corruption and honey was likely to ferment. Thus in an offering to God there must be no sign or suggestion of impurity. However, an exception must be noted as to the use of leaven and honey when offering "first-fruits" (Ch. 2:12). These first-fruits were not offered on the altar. God does allow us to present to Him this token of our devotion, even when our service is not free from imperfection.

The part of the meal offering which was burnt on the altar was only a small part of the whole. It was taken from the hand of the worshiper by the priest and burnt as "a memorial" to the Lord; the remainder of this offering was given to the priest as his support; his ministry was absolutely necessary if offerings were to be made. This essential and necessary office of the priest is further emphasized in the "supplemental ritual" for this offering (Ch. 6:14-23). Here it is prescribed that a meal offering shall be presented by the priest for the whole people of Israel every morning and every evening. This was to be a "perpetual" offering. Thus it is that our Great High Priest, who alone has fulfilled all that the "meal offering" symbolized, now exercises His continual ministry. He appears in the presence of God for us. In view of His offering we, His people, are accepted of God, not only in our persons, but in all our works.

THE PEACE OFFERING. [Chs. 3:1-17 and 7:11-38]

Fellowship is an essential feature of worship. It is this feature which in particular is pictured by the "peace offering," also called the "thank offering"; for, according to the ritual, part of this offering was laid on the altar and burnt as a gift to the Lord, part was given to the priests, and the remainder was eaten by the worshiper. The offering consisted of a bullock, a sheep or a goat. It was presented by the offerer, with the laying on of hands, and was killed on the south side of the altar; then its blood was sprinkled on the altar.

The most valuable part of the animal, the "fat," *belonged to God.* It thus had a peculiar sanctity and could not be eaten. Nor could blood be eaten. The closing words of the chapter were specific: "All the fat is the Lord's. It shall be a perpetual statute for you throughout your generations, that ye shall eat neither fat nor blood" (vs. 16, 17).

In the supplemental ritual of the Peace Offering (Ch. 7:22-27) this strict prohibition was solemnly repeated and emphasized: "For whoever eateth the fat of the beast, of which men offer an offering made by fire unto the Lord, even the soul that eateth it shall be cut off from his people. . . . And whosoever it be that eateth any blood, that soul shall be cut off from his people." The reason why blood could not be used as food was this: in it was "the life of the flesh" (Ch. 17:11, 12), and the appointed means of expiation for sin. It belonged to God. So in partaking of his daily food the Israelite was reminded that atonement by the offering of a life was the ground of acceptance with God, and, further, that the very best we possess belongs to God.

The portions of the Peace Offering which were given to the *priests* were known as the "wave breast" and the "heave shoulder." The former was held horizontally and waved toward the altar and backward from the altar to show that the part had been offered to God but now was given back by Him to the priest. So the "heave offering" was lifted up and down, presented to Jehovah, and received again from Him. This was an illustration of a principle, stated again in the New Testament, that as those who ministered of old in the office of priest were given a part of the Peace Offering so those who serve as ministers of the Gospel are rightfully supported by the free-will offerings of God's people (I Corinthians 9:13, 14).

The remainder of the "peace offering," indeed the main portion, was eaten as a joyful sacrificial feast by the *offerer* and *his family* and *his friends*. This seems to have been the supreme significance of this sacrifice. It expressed joy and peace and gratitude, but also "sharing," joint participation, fellowship and friendship. Such ever are the characteristics of true worship. This was easily understood by the Israelites, and it is not difficult to draw a comparison with the experience of Christians. Christ the Lamb of God has been given for the food of the soul, and as we partake of Him we have fellowship with God, and with one another. Thus John declares: "That which we have seen and heard declare we unto you, that ye also may have fellowship with us: and truly our fellowship is with the Father, and with his Son Jesus Christ." Rejoicing in the acceptance we have through Christ, we hold true communion with our fellow worshipers and with God.

THE SIN OFFERING. [Chs. 4:1 to 5:13 and 6:24-30]

The message of the Sin Offering was that of *expiation*. It was a gracious message, for it spoke of the provision whereby sinful man could be pardoned and brought into fellowship with a holy God.

Yet it was a solemn message, for it declared that atonement for guilt could be made only by the sacrifice of a life; it emphasized the truth that "without shedding of blood there is no remission of sin." It was the more solemn in that the provision for pardon was limited to sins of a certain class; for more serious offenses no provision was made. One who sinned in "ignorance," or rashly or without deliberate intention, or who was guilty of an injury for which full restitution might be made, could bring his offering and make his confession and receive forgiveness; but one who sinned willfully, presumptuously, "with high hand," in open rebellion against God, must suffer the penalty of death: "He that despised Moses' law died without mercy under two or three witnesses" (Hebrews 10:28).

The justice of God was shown, in that degrees of guilt were thus recognized. Not all sins are equally heinous. There may be extenuating circumstances. Our ignorance, or passion, or weakness may palliate our guilt; yet guilt remains, and can be removed only by presenting a sacrifice with penitence and confession. The Sin Offering faintly foreshadowed the atoning work of Christ; yet the fact that for the Israelite there was no possible offering which could atone for murder or adultery or blasphemy or "presumptuous" sins was also a witness to the need of a truer Sacrifice, a Sin Offering, a Saviour, through whom atonement would be possible for all sins, and by faith in whom there would be pardon for "the chief of sinners."

The "sin offerings" were of different kinds, according to the rank and responsibility of the offender. The "anointed *priest*," that is, the "high priest," must bring "a young bullock without blemish." For a sin in which the whole nation was involved a similar sacrifice was required. A ruler who had sinned must present a goat, and one of the common people must bring a kid or a lamb. However, for certain specified offenses particular regulations were enforced. A person who refused to testify in order to shield an offender, or who was ceremonially unclean, or who was guilty of a rash vow, might present a kid or a lamb, but if too poor might offer two turtle-doves or two young pigeons. If even this was too great an expense, he could offer a measure of fine flour; yet, to distinguish it from the "meal offering," this flour was not to be mixed with oil or incense.

It never must be supposed that these grades of offerings to be presented by offenders indicate that there are different standards of morality; what is wrong for a priest is wrong for a prince; however, there are degrees of responsibility corresponding with the rank and position of the persons concerned. The sin of a ruler, because of his wide influence, might create a greater scandal and bring more reproach on the name of God than the sin of a private individual. Yet in either case guilt has been incurred and can be expiated only by presenting the required offering. No person is so obscure that his sin is overlooked, none so prominent that his fault can be condoned.

This distinction between offenders was also marked by the *ritual* of the Sin Offering. In every case the offender presented his sacrifice, confessed his sin, and placed his hands on the head of the victim. This *imposition of hands* indicated that the worshiper identified himself with the sacrifice, and transferred his guilt to the offering, the life of which was to be given in his place. When the sacrifice had been slain, some of the blood was poured out at the base of the brazen altar, some sprinkled in the tabernacle before the veil, some placed on the horns of the altar of incense or on the horns of the brazen altar, or taken into the Holy of Holies and sprinkled on the mercy-seat. These methods of *sprinkling the blood* distinguished the different classes of offenders. When the High Priest had sinned, his offense defiled the Holy Place where he ministered, and when the "whole congregation" sinned, the High Priest was involved as a member of the congregation; therefore, in both cases, the Holy Place needed to be cleansed by sprinkled blood. When a ruler or one of the common people sinned, the blood of sacrifice was placed on the horns of the altar which stood in the outer court of the tabernacle, in which court ruler and people were wont to worship; by the blood of their offerings this court was cleansed. Once a year, on the Great Day of Atonement, the blood of the sin offering, which had been sacrificed for the whole nation, was taken within the veil and sprinkled on the mercy-seat above the tables of the law, thus to make atonement for the sins of the whole nation.

In the New Testament the full meaning of this "sprinkled blood" is found in the atoning sacrifice of

Christ. As Christians we are come "to the blood of sprinkling, that speaketh better things than that of Abel" (Hebrews 12:24). The blood of Abel cried from the ground for vengeance, the blood of Christ speaks of pardon and forgiveness, as we are "now justified through his blood" (Romans 5:9), and have been chosen of God unto "sprinkling of the blood of Jesus Christ" (I Peter 1:2).

The varying provisions for *the disposal of the bodies* mark another great difference in the classes of sin offerings. The fat and the most valuable portions were always burned on the brazen altar as an offering of "sweet savour" to God; but the flesh of sacrifices presented by rulers or members of the congregation was given to be eaten by priests, and the bodies of the other sin offerings were burned outside the camp.

The *peculiar sanctity* of the sin offering was emphasized by the provision that anything which was touched by the portion which belonged to the priests should be regarded as holy, every garment on which a spot of the blood was found be washed, and every vessel used in the sacrificial meal be either destroyed or thoroughly cleansed.

The main portion of these sacrifices, therefore, was carried "forth without the camp unto a clean place" and burned with fire. This provision was required, not, as some have supposed, because the offering was so associated with sin that it was regarded as unclean and so could not be consumed in the court of the tabernacle. This offering was "most holy," as has been noted. It was burned "outside the camp" to distinguish it from the burnt offering. Both were holy, but their meaning might have been confused. One symbolized dedication, the other expiation. Both were acceptable to God.

Both were figures of Christ. He offered himself in

complete consecration to the will of God, in life and in death, and also took the place of sinful man. As our substitute He "bore our sins in his own body on the tree." He was made to be "sin for us," yet Himself was not made sinful. Imputation of guilt does not impart guilt or moral imperfection. It implies liability to punishment. The sinless Son of God bore the penalty due to our sins. He was so identified with us that He was treated as we deserve. Yet in Him was no fault; He "knew no sin." This peculiar holiness of the "sin offering" needs to be emphasized in every reference to the divine Sin Bearer. He who suffered for our sins was at the same time "most holy." Never was He more truly beloved of His Father than at the moment when He cried, "Why hast thou forsaken me?" He could at once breathe out His spirit with the prayer, "Father into thy hands I commend my spirit." He was accepted of His Father, and by faith in Him we have forgiveness and are accepted by God.

The ritual of the "sin offering" conveys another important lesson. Let us review it as we find it recorded in the Epistle to the Hebrews: "We have an altar"—the cross on which Christ died and there made atonement for us—"whereof they have no right to eat which serve the tabernacle," that is, those who still trust in rites and ceremonies, or in their own good deeds, to secure their salvation; "for the bodies of those beasts whose blood is brought into the sanctuary by the high priest for sin are burned without the camp. Wherefore Jesus also, that he might sanctify the people with his own blood, suffered without the gate"—the gate of the city, the gate of Judaism, rejected by His own people, given into the hands of Gentiles to be crucified. "Let us therefore go forth to him without the camp, bearing his reproach" as those who no longer belong to Judaism, or to any religion of rites and ceremonies, and forms and self-righteousness—to any people who deny the efficacy of the Sin Offering, or the message of the cross. Yet as priests at a new altar we are privileged to present a spiritual ritual. "By him therefore let us offer the sacrifice of praise to God continually. . . . But to do good and to communicate forget not; for with such sacrifices God is well pleased" (Hebrews 13:10-16).

THE TRESPASS OFFERING.
[Chs. 5:14 to 6:7 and 7:1-10]

As the "burnt offering" symbolized dedication, and the "peace offering" symbolized communion, and the "sin offering" expiation, so the "trespass" or "guilt offering" symbolized *satisfaction* or restitution. It may be regarded as a particular kind of sin offering, or better still as an offering for a particular kind of sin. The offense to which it was related consisted in invading or disregarding the property rights of another person. Thus every trespass was a sin but not every sin was a trespass. Therefore, expiation was to be made because the trespass was a sin, but satisfaction or reparation of the wrong was to be made because the sin was also a trespass.

In every case and for all persons, the trespass offering was in the form of a ram. This differed from the ritual of the sin offering, where there was a graduation of sacrifices according to the degree of guilt and responsibility, and also according to the wealth or poverty of the offender. Another distinguishing feature was the required payment of full reparation for the trespass, and an additional fine of one-fifth, that is, two-tenths, of the whole amount involved. This, indeed, may be regarded as the essential characteristic of the trespass offering.

There were two classes of these offerings. One related to the "holy things of the Lord" (Ch. 5:14-19), the other to violations of the property rights of men (Ch. 6:1-7). The "holy things" included tithes and offerings and property given in vows. If the offense was committed in ignorance, and its amount subsequently learned, full restitution must be made, and a fifth part added. However, a ram first must be offered as a sacrifice; for even full restitution could not restore fellowship with God. A sin had been committed, and even though it had been "in ignorance" the sin required sacrifice, for "without shedding of blood is no remission of sin."

If the offense had been committed in ignorance, and the amount of the trespass could not be ascertained, obviously no equivalent restitution could be made, but, nevertheless, the sacrifice must be offered in order that communion with God could be restored.

The people of God today need to be reminded that God has certain rights in their property. A man may "rob God" in "tithes and offerings" (Malachi 3:8, 9). All of us owe debts of obedience and service which need to be pardoned and repaid.

As to the second class of trespasses, those relating to men, several specific examples are given (Ch. 6:1-7). The first is a "matter of deposit," which one man has entrusted to another for safe-keeping, and which has been lost carelessly or disposed of dishonestly. The second is a "bargain" when one takes advantage of another's ignorance or need, and so secures property unfairly and for less than its value.

Another is named "robbery"; it includes not merely

deeds of violence, but any act by which a man unfairly secures possession of the property of his neighbor. Then there is *"oppression,"* "grinding the faces of the poor," giving for one's labor less than justice demands. Last, mention is made of one who has *"found* that which was *lost* and lieth concerning it, and sweareth falsely."

All these offenses have surprisingly familiar and modern parallels and applications. These are among the common ways in which the rights of others are being invaded. The followers of Christ need to learn and to practice the lesson of the "trespass offering." If we are guilty of offending another person, it is not enough for us to feel repentant, and to ask God for forgiveness. We must confess to the person we have offended and ask for pardon; but we must do more than this; we must make full and complete reparation for the injury we have done; and we must do this first, before we ask God for pardon, or expect His forgiveness. This changed order of the ritual is deeply significant. When one had committed a trespass in "the holy things of the Lord," he first presented his offering to God, and then made any possible restitution; but when one had trespassed against his fellow man, he first made reparation, with the added penalty of a double tithe, and he then approached God with his offering. Let us remember this message, and, first of all, seek to repair any injury to our fellow man before we ask for pardon and expect to renew our fellowship with God.

Pardon can be expected if we come to God in the name of Christ, who is the perfect Trespass Offering. In Him the prophetic symbol finds its fulfilment. He was made "an offering for sin" (Isaiah 53:10), literally "a trespass offering." This reference indicates that to this offering the highest degree of efficacy was ascribed. As

the Trespass Offering, Christ not only expiated sin, He
also restored, He redeemed, He made complete reparation.
We may be conscious of how much we owe to God, of
how great our debt is to Him, of how imperfect our service has been, of how we have "robbed him in tithes and
offerings," and in rightful devotion; but we come to Him
in the name of Christ, by whom complete satisfaction has
been made, and we believe that we are "accepted in the
Beloved." He is the Perfect Sacrifice. He is not only our
Trespass Offering, but He is the Substance of which all
the Levitical Offerings were shadows and types. By
Him complete atonement has been made. Through Him
eternal salvation has been secured.

PRIESTHOOD. [Chs. 8 to 10]

As the worshiper approached God he needed not
only an offering (Chs. 1 to 7), but also the *mediation* of a
priest. We now are assured that "there is one God, and
one mediator between God and men, the man Christ
Jesus" (I Timothy 2:5). By Him free and unrestricted
access to God is given to all believers, at all places and
times. To place any mediator, any sacrament, any church
between Him and a human soul is to deny His claims and
to detract from His glory. Of Him, Aaron, brother of
Moses, High Priest of Israel, was a type. As the sons of
Aaron were likewise priests and assisted Aaron in his
work, so the followers of Christ form a "universal priesthood of believers." They can pray for their fellow men;
they can offer sacrifices of praise; they can promise pardon
to all who accept and believe; they can lead in worship
and bring others into fellowship with God. From among
their number they select certain ones who are trained and

qualified and chosen to conduct public worship, to give religious instruction, to lead in the work of congregations; but these are "ministers," that is, "servants." They should not form a separate caste, they have no spiritual privileges or rights which are not shared by their fellow believers. All believers are on an equality before God and have the same rank as members of the "royal priesthood"; all of them have access to God, through faith in Christ.

We should seek to discover what messages are conveyed in the account of the ancient *priesthood* (Chs. 8 to 10). These chapters form the only historical section of the Book of Leviticus, excepting the few verses in Chapter 24:10-23. This section contains the account of the consecration of the priests (Ch. 8), the inauguration of the tabernacle service (Ch. 9), and the solemn warning as to the sanctity of the divinely appointed worship (Ch. 10).

The Consecration of Aaron and his Sons (Ch. 8). This was in exact accordance with the ritual prescribed by God and recorded in the Book of Exodus (Chs. 29 and 40). The narrative is an important link between these two inspired books. Everything is done in accordance with divine arrangement. The fact is recorded twelve times in this single chapter.

The ceremony was conducted by Moses, as God's representative. It was held at the entrance to the Tabernacle in the presence of the people. "And Moses said unto the congregation, This is the thing which the Lord commanded to be done" (v. 5).

It might be noted, first of all, that Aaron and his sons were divinely *chosen*. They were not priests by birth or inheritance or by popular election. This is likewise true of Christ and His followers. As the author of Hebrews declares concerning the high priest, "No man taketh this honor unto himself, but he that is called of God, as was Aaron. So also Christ glorified not himself to be made an high priest; but he that said unto him, Thou art my Son, today have I begotten thee" (Hebrews 5:4, 5). So Christians, in mere grace, are "chosen" and "called" to their high office and sacred service (I Peter 1:2; Jude 1; Ephesians 1:4, 5).

As the ceremony begins, the priests are *cleansed*: "And Moses brought Aaron and his sons, and washed them with water" (v. 6). One cannot fail to be reminded of the spotless purity of Christ, our Great High Priest: "For such an high priest became us, who is holy, harmless, undefiled, separate from sinners" (Hebrews 7:26). Also as the sons of Aaron required this ceremonial cleansing, so all who are called to be priests unto God, as followers of Christ, require a moral and spiritual purification, namely, the "washing of regeneration" (Titus 3:5). They must be sanctified and cleansed "with the washing of water by the word" (Ephesians 5:26). While they still may need daily cleansing from daily defilement, they have been "bathed" once for all when by faith they entered on their Christian life. As the Master declared, "He that is bathed needeth not to save wash his feet but is clean every whit" (John 13:10 R.V.).

In the next act of consecration, Aaron and his sons were *clothed* (vs. 7-9, 13). The garments "for glory and beauty" placed on Aaron probably surpassed in magnificence even the gorgeous robes worn by the priests of papal or imperial Rome. Each article was prepared in accordance with specified divine instructions (Exodus 28). Each must have had some symbolic reference to Christ. Possibly it is sufficient here to be reminded of the matchless spiritual "glory" and moral "beauty" manifested by our

Great High Priest. As the "sons of Aaron" were clothed in white linen, we are pointed at once to the "fine linen" which is "the righteousness of saints" (Revelation 19:8). Christians not only are to be cleansed from evil habits and dispositions; they must manifest also positive virtues and lives of "beauty" if they are to minister to their fellow men as priests of God.

Aaron and his sons, as also the tablernacle, were then *anointed* with oil (vs. 10-12, 30). This was to signify that not only the priests, but the very place where they ministered was consecrated to God. As oil is the recognized symbol of the Holy Spirit, this ceremony indicated that only by the power and influence of His Spirit can worship be rendered which will be acceptable to God. The anointing of Aaron (vs. 12) differed from the application of oil to his sons (v. 30). In the case of the high priest the oil was poured on his head so abundantly that it "ran down upon his beard" and "went down to the skirts of his garments" (Psalm 133:2). However, the oil was merely "sprinkled" on the sons of Aaron and their garments. Thus we are told that the Spirit "was not given by measure" to Christ (John 3:34). He was the "Messiah," that is, the "Anointed One." He was "anointed with the Holy Ghost and with power" (Acts 10:38). So His followers, in a lesser measure, but in reality, "have an anointing" (an "unction") from the Holy One (I John 2:20). It is only by the power of His Spirit that we can render true service to God or worship acceptably in His sanctuary.

The consecration sacrifices form the closing and most significant feature of the ceremony. These various offerings represented *dedication* on the part of the priests, and *acceptance* on the part of God. At this time alone Moses

officiated, since the consecration of Aaron as yet had not
been completed. First of all, he presented a *"sin offering,"* for, excepting our sinless Saviour, all who are to be
set apart for priestly service need pardon and expiation for
guilt, and without such an offering the ritual for ordination would not have been complete. The offering was a
bullock. The most valuable parts were burned on the
altar. The remainder was burned "without the camp."

Moses next brought a ram for a *"burnt offering."* As
it was wholly consumed on the altar and was an "offering
made by fire unto the Lord," it symbolized the fact that
Aaron and his sons were completely dedicated to the
Lord. In such complete dedication Christians are to
imitate the example of their Great High Priest in absolute devotion to the will of God.

In the ceremony of the *"peace offering"* a peculiar
feature was introduced in the use made of the blood. A
portion was placed on the right ear of Aaron, a portion on
his right hand and a portion on his right foot. This likewise was done to each of Aaron's sons. Thus it was indicated that in view of the blood which has been shed, one
who is truly serving God must be ready to hear His word,
to undertake His work, and to run at His command.

The prescribed portions of this offering were burned
on the altar; but most of the flesh was used for a sacrificial
feast. A part of the offering belonged to Moses, but the
rest was eaten by Aaron and his sons "at the door of
the tabernacle of the congregation." This feast was to
indicate gratitude to God for choosing them to be His
priests, fellowship with Him and with one another as
His servants, and, most of all, the impartation of strength
for their tasks as they were fed from the altar. Such
messages come to all Christians when, a company of

priests, they gather to celebrate the sacrifice of Christ, to commune with one another, and by faith to identify themselves with Him, thus receiving new strength for their spiritual service.

For seven days Aaron and his sons were confined continually to the tabernacle, and each day the solemn ceremonies were repeated. This was not only to emphasize the importance of the ceremonies, but particularly to indicate that the very essence of consecration consists in *separation*. Aaron and his sons were so confined lest they be rendered ceremonially unclean by contact with the unclean, and so become unfitted for service. So Christ prayed that His followers would be "kept" from "evil" and thus consecrated and "sanctified" (John 17:15, 17). It is for them to endeavor to avoid the evil that is in the world, and so ever to be qualified for their exalted tasks as priests of the Most High God.

Such an elaborate ceremony of consecration (Ch. 8) is replete with messages for Christians. They are not only chosen, cleansed, clothed, anointed, dedicated and strengthened, but also separated for the service of Christ as a royal priesthood. However, the chief import of this chapter is the fulfilment of its types and symbols, not so much as these appear in relation to the sons of Aaron, but more impressively as related to the high priest, and as they are fulfilled in Christ. This chapter concerned with priesthood turns us in reverence toward Him in new devotion and trust, as the exhortation is phrased by the author of the Hebrews: "Having, therefore, brethren, boldness to enter into the holiest, by the blood of Jesus . . . and having an high priest over the house of God; let us draw near with a true heart in full assurance of faith, having our hearts sprinkled from an evil conscience, and

our bodies washed with pure water. Let us hold fast the
profession of our faith without wavering; (for he is faithful that promised)" (Hebrews 10:19-23).

THE INAUGURATION OF THE TABERNACLE
SERVICE. [Ch. 9]

One who would understand how sinful man can approach a holy God and be acceptable to Him must study
the ninth chapter of Leviticus. It is a chapter of history
and records the ceremony by which the solemn ordination of the Hebrew priests was brought to its climax and
its close. Still more, it describes the opening service of
worship in the Tabernacle, which was to supply the form
to be followed by the priests of Israel in the years to come.
What is yet more important, this service was symbolic of
the way of worship and of that fellowship with God
which can be enjoyed by all who put their trust in Christ
as their Great High Priest, their Mediator and their Lord.

The Tabernacle itself was a symbolic structure. This
"Tent of Meeting" was not a place where worshipers
could meet one another, but a shrine in which representatives of the people could meet with God. In the first of
its two small compartments, the "Holy Place," stood the
golden lampstand (the "candlestick"), the table of shew
bread, and the altar of incense. In the second, the "Holy
of Holies," was the ark and the mercy seat, above which
the cloud of glory indicated the divine Presence. Surrounding the tent was an open court in which was placed
the Brazen Altar and the Laver. This court could be
entered by priests and people when sacrifices were to be
offered. To the Holy Place only the ministering priests
were admitted. Into the Holy of Holies the high priest

alone could enter, and only once a year. Thus the Tabernacle represented what the New Testament interpreted as lessons both of restriction and of privilege. The privilege was that of worship, of approach to God, and of fellowship with Him; but this privilege was limited to certain times and persons and was possible only under certain conditions. These conditions are set forth in the ritual prescribed in the Book of Leviticus. This included offerings to secure atonement, and the mediation of priests. When these offerings had been specified (Chs. 1-7), and when a priesthood had been established (Ch. 8), a service was conducted which could be regarded as a model to be followed at all subsequent times, and in which the people of God in all ages would find instruction as to the principles and laws of divine worship (Ch. 9).

This service was conducted at the "door of the Tabernacle," in the presence of the "elders" who represented the people, and who are identified in the narrative with "the children of Israel." The divine arrangement was dictated by Moses to Aaron (vs. 1-6). It included the specific sacrifices which were to be presented by Aaron, first for himself and then for the people. It is surprising that Aaron needed to bring a "sin offering." He already had been washed and clothed and anointed for service. Yet it is true that all who worship God, no matter what their previous spiritual experience, or how high their office, need "daily cleansing from daily defilement," and continually must rely on the efficacy of the "blood of Christ" which cleanses from all sin. The particular offering required of Aaron was "a young calf." This was absolutely unique; for no other person at any time was such a sacrifice specified. It is possible that the

conjecture is correct according to which there was a re-
minder of the precise sin always associated with the name
of Aaron, that is, his preparing a golden calf to be wor-
shiped by the people of Israel. Aaron was required also
to present a "ram for a burnt offering." This offering, it
will be remembered, was a symbol of complete consecration. Thus, when any worshiper is to enter on a new act
or sphere of service, he should offer himself anew in complete consecration to God.

For the people, in addition to a sin offering and a
burnt offering, there were to be presented "peace offerings, to sacrifice before the Lord," since worship includes
the praise and gladness and fellowship which the peace
offering symbolized. The goal or climax of worship is a
clearer spiritual vision of God. So in the brief instructions given by Moses to Aaron is repeated twice the
inspiring promise, "Today the Lord will appear unto you"
(v. 4), and "the glory of the Lord shall appear unto you"
(v. 6).

With these instructions in mind, Aaron conducted
the solemn initial service of worship in the Tabernacle.
The significant and instructive feature of the ritual then
established was the *order of the offerings*, first the offering
for sin, then the burnt and meal offerings, and then the
peace offering. There is no other order possible for any
worshiper at any time or place. The sin offering always
must come first. No one ever can approach God without
confession of guilt and unworthiness and without reli-
ance on the precious blood of Christ. Then can follow
the burnt offering with its accompanying meal offering,
that is, the dedication of self and also the dedication of
one's toil. Such dedication is accepted only of those
who come trusting in the atoning work of Christ; indeed,

such trust is the inspiration and motive for complete surrender to the will and service of the Lord: "Because we thus judge, that one died for all . . . and he died for all, that they that live should no longer live unto themselves, but unto him who for their sakes died and rose again" (II Corinthians 5:14, 15).

The peace offering, with its symbolism of joy and of fellowship with God and with one another, will come last. The order cannot be reversed. One cannot expect peace and gladness and new strength until there has been surrender to Christ and confidence in His redeeming grace. Consecration is sure to be followed by the feast of fellowship, and then by the new vision, such as was granted to the worshipers of old: "And the glory of the Lord appeared unto all the people" (v. 23). Some new splendor seems to have shown forth from the cloud which rested on the Holy of Holies.

This appearance, however, was preceded by the two-fold benediction which concluded the Tabernacle service, "Aaron lifted up his hand toward the people and blessed them" (v. 22). There is little doubt that his words were those which have become familiar to all the people of God, and which are associated with the office of the high priest: "The Lord bless thee and keep thee; the Lord make his face to shine upon thee, and be gracious unto thee; the Lord lift up his countenance upon thee, and give thee peace."

After these words of blessing, "Moses and Aaron went into the tabernacle of the congregation." Aaron may have had much to learn from Moses in the Holy Place, about the worship of the "golden candle-stick," the table of shew-bread and the altar of incense. At that altar they were before the veil and in the immediate presence

of God. Then, as they came out, they "blessed the
people; and the glory of the Lord appeared unto all the
people" (v. 23).

Many readers find a beautiful analogy between this
double benediction and the ministry of our blessed Lord.
Whenever we meet to worship in His name we may catch
some vision of His grace and mercy and may receive some
new benediction of peace; but when He ascended He
blessed His disciples and disappeared into the unseen,
and as He now intercedes on high for His followers, so
some day He will appear again to bring a fuller blessing
and we shall see Him face to face.

As "the glory of the Lord appeared unto all the
people . . . there came a fire out from before the Lord
and consumed upon the altar the burnt offering and the
fat; which when all the people saw, they shouted, and
fell on their faces" (v. 24). Thus, too, at the conclusion
of every period of true worship there may be in the experience of the worshipers a sense of divine acceptance and
a hymn of praise to God.

THE SIN OF NADAB AND ABIHU. [Ch. 10]

A most solemn sanction was given to the form of worship which had been divinely ordained and had been
observed by Moses and Aaron. The event is recorded as
follows: "And Nadab and Abihu, the sons of Aaron, took
each of them his censer, and put fire therein, and laid
incense thereon, and offered strange fire before Jehovah,
which he had not commanded them. And there came
forth fire before Jehovah, and devoured them, and they
died before Jehovah" (Ch. 10:1, 2).

The exact sin of which Nadab and Abihu were guilty

is not definitely known. Some suppose that they introduced into the incense ingredients not included in the specific directions for its preparation (Exodus 30:34-38); or that they had used fire other than that furnished by "coals from off the altar" (Ch. 16:12).

Others have concluded that the incense was offered at a time not prescribed in the order of worship just established, and not as a morning or evening sacrifice. Others object that the two men together offered incense, whereas it should have been offered by one priest at one time. Nadab and Abihu used their own censers and not the sacred vessels of the sanctuary, whereas the use of the censer was confined to the high priest alone. Most serious of all is the view that these two priests rashly penetrated into the Holy of Holies, which the high priest alone could enter, and he only on the Day of Atonement.

Whatever the exact nature of the sin, their action was that of presumptuous self-will, and this too in a ceremony for which they had received specific commands from God. Their motive may have been innocent. They may have intended to render worship and adoration, but their sin was just as real, "and there came out fire from the Lord and devoured them." Men are slow to learn that "to obey is better than sacrifice," that submission to the divine will is sweeter than incense. Even today much that is regarded as worship is really "strange fire." In pagan lands there are rites and ceremonies which are contrary to the laws of God, and even among Christians there are forms and practices for which no sanction can be found in divine revelation. It is a very serious matter for one to approach God with no dependence on the mediating atoning work of Christ, or to present merely the "meal offering" consisting in the work of one's own hands and good deeds, with no thought of a sacrifice for sin.

To Aaron, the heart-broken father, Moses interprets the meaning of this tragic event. He quotes a divine communication previously received, but until now not recorded: "Then Moses said unto Aaron, This is that the Lord spake, saying, I will be sanctified in them that come nigh me, and before all the people I will be glorified" (v. 3). The words, "them that come nigh me," were, in the first instance, addressed to the priests, but the message is for all who approach God as worshipers. The greater the privilege, the greater the responsibility. The priests had been ordained so that by their service they might teach the holiness of God; if by their sin they failed in this high duty, still the holiness of God would be shown by the very punishment inflicted upon them. To this word there could be no answer; from such a judgment there could be no appeal, "And Aaron held his peace."

This submissive silence on the part of Aaron is in harmony with the restriction and the provision for mourning which Moses now enjoins. The bodies of Nadab and Abihu, still shrouded in their priestly garments, were to be carried without the camp for burial. The distress of acting as bearers was spared the two surviving brothers, and the sad rite was performed by their cousins. All the people of Israel were permitted to express their sorrow and distress and to "bewail the burning which the Lord had kindled." Aaron and his sons, however, were to show no such signs of sorrow as might interrupt their priestly service. They were not to dishevel their hair nor to rend their garments, nor to show the customary signs of grief. The reason assigned by Moses was this: "The anointing oil of the Lord has been upon you." That is to say, they

had been ordained as the representatives of God. Therefore, when God had shown His wrath against sin, for
them to mourn in public for this divine action would
seem to contradict their sacred calling. They were bidden
to remain in the seclusion of the sanctuary while the
people mourned and while their relatives performed the
sad rites for the burial of the dead. It is only very rarely
that expressions of affection are in conflict with sacred
duty, but where human sympathy would prompt one to
neglect a task or a course of action clearly and definitely
assigned, then the most tender of human ties must not
be allowed to turn one from the duty which he has accepted from God.

Just at this point in the narrative is introduced the
prohibition against the use of wine: "And the Lord spake
unto Aaron, saying, Do not drink wine nor strong drink,
thou, nor thy sons with thee, when ye go into the tabernacle of the congregation, lest ye die: it shall be a statute
for ever throughout your generations" (Ch. 10:8, 9).

The purpose of this prohibition is added: "And that
ye may put difference between holy and unholy, and between unclean and clean; and that ye may teach the
children of Israel all the statutes which the Lord hath
spoken unto them by the hand of Moses" (Ch. 10:10,
11). From the immediate connection of this prohibition
with the sin of Nadab and Abihu, it has been concluded
that it was under the influence of wine that these men
committed their rash sacrilege. This is quite probable,
but not absolutely certain, nor are the words to be interpreted to mean that God forbade the use of wine to all
men or even to priests at all times. Yet this was a solemn
warning. The use of wine might so confuse the mind as
to incapacitate the priests for their sacred service. They

might not be able to distinguish so clearly "between the holy and unholy and between unclean and clean," just as today a first effect of alcohol is to blunt the moral sense and to dull the perception of the difference between right and wrong. Christians form a "priesthood of believers"; it is their duty to avoid any practice which may stand in the way of their high service or to put to risk the full performance of their sacred duties. It is their privilege to do all in their power to discourage the use of beverages which result in conduct as rash and fatal as that of Nadab and Abihu.

While Aaron obeyed Moses in refraining from all public manifestation of grief for the death of his two sons, he adopted one course of action in the seclusion of the Tabernacle which received the censure of Moses. He and his two remaining sons refrained from eating the flesh of the sin offerings which properly belonged to them as officiating priests. "Ye should indeed have eaten it in the holy place as I commanded," was the rebuke of Moses. To this Aaron made his notable reply, "Behold this day have they offered their sin offering and their burnt offering before the Lord; and such things have befallen me: and if I had eaten the sin offering today, should it have been accepted in the sight of the Lord?" His defense, then, was this: In spite of their deep sorrow his sons had continued their priestly service. They had "offered their sin offering and their burnt offering before the Lord"; but a terrible calamity had come upon Aaron: "Such things have befallen me." Nadab and Abihu had been guilty of mortal sin. Since he was their father he felt implicated in their crime. While he could offer sacrifices, he could not partake of the flesh which was accounted "most holy." So Aaron concludes: "If I had eaten the sin offering today, should it have been accepted in the sight of the Lord?" He had not kept the letter of the law, but he had shown himself keenly sensitive to its spirit. By his action he had revealed the secret of his soul; he had realized the holiness of God, demonstrated by the penalty inflicted on his sons, and he was confessing his own unworthiness as a priest of the holy God. "And when Moses heard that, he was content." He realized that his own rebuke of Aaron had been hasty and undeserved.

Thus as the scene closes after this tragic event, the two famous brothers, Moses and Aaron, appear in a truly noble attitude of humility and meekness, and show themselves worthy to be regarded as the leaders and the high priests of the people of God.

II

THE REQUISITE FOR WORSHIP
LEVITICUS 11 to 22

LEVITICUS is a handbook for worshipers, and its key word is *holiness*. Again and again this term is repeated. The thought molds every paragraph. The opening chapters deal with holy offerings and a holy priesthood (Chs. 1-10). The section following concerns ceremonial holiness (Chs. 11-16). The remainder of the book is often designated "The Law of Holiness" (Chs. 17-26); it concerns holiness in daily life and the holiness of sacred seasons. This is followed by an "appendix," which deals with the holiness of vows (Ch. 27). However the book may be analyzed, it evidently teaches that holiness is the supreme requirement in worship. Sacrifices and priesthood are of no avail unless there is purity of heart and life on the part of those who have fellowship with God.

What, then, is meant by holiness? The root of the Hebrew word usually is understood to denote "separation." As related to God, it implied His freedom from all creature imperfections and limitations in His infinite power and righteousness and love. As applied to objects or times or places, it indicated those which have been separated from common use and dedicated to the service of God; but, further, as applied to men, it denoted such moral and spiritual character and conduct as became those who had been separated from evil and dedicated to God. So, in the New Testament, a similar word is used to describe Christians, who are designated as "saints" or "holy ones." They have been separated from the world, and, as servants of Christ, are supposed to manifest those virtues which are in harmony with their high calling.

Thus "holiness," in the Book of Leviticus, may be either ceremonial or moral. It may mean such obedience to ritual requirements as qualify one for worship (Chs. 11-16), or such purity of life as should characterize persons who are wholly yielded to God (Chs. 17-26).

PURIFICATION. *Ceremonial Holiness.*
[Chs. 11 to 16:34]

These regulations are closely related to the chapters which precede. Those chapters state the provision for access to God; these declare that one must be ceremonially clean if he desires to appropriate this provision. The chapters which then follow deal with moral purity. Both forms of holiness were required of the Israelites; both contain instruction for the followers of Christ. These earlier chapters deal with Clean and Unclean Foods (Ch. 11), with Purification after Childbirth (Ch. 12), with The Cleansing of Leprosy (Chs. 13, 14), with the Cleansing of Bodily Issues (Ch. 15), and with the Day of Atonement, the time of national purification (Ch. 16).

CLEAN AND UNCLEAN FOODS. [Ch. 11]

Severe restrictions were placed on Israel as to the kind of animals which could be used for food. These restrictions were not arbitrary nor absurd nor meaningless. On the contrary, they were wise and sensible and of deep significance. They were adapted to a people dwelling for forty years in a wilderness and afterward located in a small country with a tropical climate. Not all of these restrictions would apply to other nations; yet they involved principles applicable to all peoples in all times and places.

It will be remembered that these regulations were as follows:

(1) Of the large land animals, those were "clean" which had cloven hoofs and also chewed the cud. Both these conditions must be fulfilled. This, for example, would include the ox but exclude the camel, which had the latter but lacked the former of these two requirements, inasmuch as the hoof of the camel, while divided above, is united beneath in a broad sole. Thus, in general, beasts of prey were regarded as unclean (vs. 3-8).

(2) Water animals were clean if they had both fins and scales. Shellfish and eels were not to be eaten (vs. 9-12).

(3) Except rather a long list specifically named, fowls and birds were regarded as proper for food. The exceptions were largely birds of prey and such as feed on dead bodies. The exact birds indicated in the forbidden list are not in all cases recognized by their Hebrew names, and to them is added, as a winged creature, the bat (vs. 13-19).

(4) Winged creeping things are specified. Practically all are prohibited for food, except only various species of locusts (vs. 20-33).

(5) Absolutely no carrion could be eaten. Even to touch a dead body was defiling and disqualified one for the public worship of God (vs. 24-40).

(6) "All creeping things" were forbidden as food (vs. 41-44).

(7) The reason for these restrictions is the necessity for holiness on the part of the worshipers of a holy God (vs. 45-47).

Evidently one prime purpose in all these regulations of diet was the preservation of health. Natural instinct, the practice of civilized nations and the precepts of modern science all unite in confirming the wisdom of these laws. Not all the creatures proscribed are equally repulsive, not all are equally dangerous as food; but, on the whole, such specifications easily could be understood and would be safeguards against disease. Today such rules may be modified by methods of refrigeration and by various climatic conditions. For instance, the Hebrews were denied the use of fat, but in the arctic regions this now is regarded as needed to sustain life. Pork and oysters are now eaten with safety in most places, but even these are illustrations of articles easily spoiled by heat and under many conditions dangerous for food.

There can be no doubt that the purpose of the Mosaic legislation was to exclude as objects of diet those animals most liable to attack by infectious or parasitic diseases. It also should be noted that the minute directions in reference to all defilement by dead bodies (vs. 24-40) are quite in accordance with the fact that on the death of an infected animal the poisons and parasites multiply with intense rapidity.

Any careful study of the principles involved in these regulations on diet and contact with dead bodies must lead one to believe that they were designed to avoid infection and to protect bodily health. What shall be said, then, of the explicit statement that the regulations were not in the sphere of hygiene but in that of religion? The statement is made in these precise words, "For I am the Lord your God; ye shall sanctify yourselves and shall be holy; for I am holy." Is there a contradition here? On the contrary, the harmony and unity of these two aims contain an impressive and practical message. True religion concerns the body as well as the spirit. Persons are holy who are separated unto the service of God. They belong to Him. To them comes the exhortation, "Know ye not that your body is the temple of the Holy Ghost which ye have of God, and ye are not your own? For ye are bought with a price; therefore glorify God in your body, and in your spirit, which are God's" (I Corinthians 6:19, 20). True servants of the Lord will realize that it is their duty to exercise all possible care of their physical health. They know that bodily conditions influence their mental and spiritual states. Therefore, they will seek to be instruments fit for the Master's use. All injurious habits of eating and drinking will be avoided. They will seek to be holy and thus to be proper temples for the Holy Ghost.

There was a further purpose in these ancient regulations on diet. They distinguished Israel as a separate nation distinct from the idolatrous peoples about them. Whether or not this was a prime purpose, it certainly was a result. Possibly today Christians are called on to bear a more definite testimony to their Lord by their refusal to follow present social customs in the matter of eating, and particularly of drinking. They should be distinguished from others in refraining from anything which endangers or injures the body, and should regard the preservation of health as a sacred duty. They should heed the familiar word of the apostle, "Whether therefore ye

eat, or drink, or whatever ye do, do all to the glory of
God" (I Corinthians 10:31).

PURIFICATION AFTER CHILDBIRTH. [Ch. 12]

It may seem that Mount Sinai and the Mosaic laws
of purification are far removed from Bethlehem and the
story of Joseph and Mary and the Wise Men from the
East. In reality, those laws and that story are closely related. For one thing, they make it quite clear that the
Wise Men did not reach Bethlehem on the day of our
Saviour's birth. In obedience to the Mosaic statute, Mary
brought her son to Jerusalem to present Him to the Lord,
forty days after His birth. It was subsequent to this "presentation in the temple" that His parents fled to Egypt to
escape the murderous decree of Herod, who sought the
"young child to destroy him"; and this decree of the king
was directly connected with the report and the departure
of the Wise Men. However, this uncertainty as to the
exact date of the arrival of the Wise Men must not mar
for us the beauty of the Christmas scene with which we
are familiar. When we picture the birth of our Lord we
do well to introduce the star and the Wise Men quite as
truly as the angels and the shepherds. All are parts of the
Christmas scene; all are symbols of the nativity. Prosaic
exactness must not be allowed to mar the music and the
poetry which we associate with the "good tidings of great
joy."

Furthermore, this "law of purification" emphasizes
the poverty of Joseph and Mary. We think they were
poor because "there was no room for them in the inn."
Quite right, but sometimes travelers are excluded from a
crowded hostelry even when their purses are fairly well

filled. Or we might argue that their humble station in
life was due to the fact that Joseph was a "carpenter."
This also is a natural conclusion; but even in that early
day carpenters or "builders" were not necessarily poor.
The unquestioned proof of the poverty of these parents
is found in the words of the law and in the story from
the Gospel, "when the days of her purifying are fulfilled
for a son or for a daughter, she shall bring a lamb of the
first year for a burnt offering and a young pigeon or a
turtle dove for a sin offering unto the door of the congregation, unto the priest . . . and if she be not able to
bring a lamb then she shall bring two turtle doves, or
two young pigeons" (Ch. 12:6, 8).

According. to the Gospel story, Mary and Joseph
brought a pair of turtle doves: they could not afford to
bring a lamb (Luke 2:24). Those gifts of gold and
frankincense and myrrh presented by the Wise Men must
have been a providential and necessary help when the
"holy family" started in haste to sojourn for a time in
Egypt.

The supreme message of Bethlehem, however, is embodied in the name given to the Christ-child, "Thou shalt
call his name JESUS, for he shall save his people from
their sins." This is exactly the solemn message of "the
law of purification after childbirth." It is the message
which expresses the need of a Saviour. According to the
law, a woman who had given birth to a son was regarded
as unclean for seven days, and was separated from the
congregation of worshipers for forty days. No doubt the
purpose was a regard for health and for the recovery of
strength, but there was undoubtedly a deeper and symbolic meaning in the ordinance. The reference to uncleanness and purification indicates some relation to sin,

and for one to be restored to the privilege of worship, a
burnt offering and a sin offering must be provided. Let us
remember that we are dealing here with types and symbols and are concerned with ceremonial and not with
moral purity. Motherhood is a woman's very crown and
glory. Yet it is a solemn reality that every child, save
One, has been born with the taint of sin. The "Holy One
of Israel," the Son of Mary, was likewise the Son of God;
in Him was no sin; but the nature of all His brother men
was so prone to evil that one who bore such a child was
regarded as in need of *ceremonial* cleansing. The child
himself needed to be purified. Thus the rite of circum-
cision (v. 3), while designed to secure physical health
was imposed as a symbol of the putting off of sin and
uncleanness. The mother was regarded as ceremonially
unclean for forty days, then, as the law was made to read,
she must bring her offering for sin "and the priest shall
make atonement for her and she shall be clean." It
humbles our pride to be reminded of the truth that we all
are born with the imperfection and tendency to evil which
characterizes the human race. Yet God in His mercy has
provided a Saviour through whom we have "atonement"
and by whose power we are made clean. Whatever stain
or impurity our natural disposition has been allowed to
produce, "the blood of Jesus Christ, his Son, cleanseth us
from all sin." Through Christ our fellowship with God
is restored and we are accepted as true worshipers.

THE CLEANSING OF LEPROSY. [Chs. 13 and 14]

Leprosy is commonly regarded as the most terrible of
the diseases by which the human body is tortured and destroyed. It has appeared in different forms. The most

horrible has borne the difficult name of *Elephantiasis Græcorum* ("elephant disease of the Greeks"). In its worst character it appears in circular spots on various parts of the body. It soon spreads. Later the joints are affected and fall apart, producing mutilation, pitiful deformity, and death. The more common form of leprosy is that of a skin disease known as *Psoriasis Vulgaris*. It is much less serious and does not endanger the life of the sufferer. While it is difficult to determine the exact nature of the leprosy described in Leviticus, it was evidently much more than an affliction of the skin; yet on the other hand, it was not always incurable, as the more desperate forms are understood to have been. No repulsive and cruel symptoms are described, possibly because these chapters deal with the earlier stages of the malady. Whatever the exact form of this dread disease may have been, it was commonly taken as a symbol of the loathsomeness and isolation and destructiveness of sin.

While such a comparison is arresting and instructive, two facts should be borne in mind: first, this striking analogy is not specified in Scripture; and, second, while in the Old Testament memorable examples are recorded of sin being punished by the infliction of leprosy, as in the cases of Miriam and Gehazi and Uzziah, one must be very careful lest any statement be made which might be interpreted to suggest that a person suffering today from leprosy has been guilty of some moral fault. The most pitiful leper may be the moral and spiritual equal of anyone who is in perfect physical health. Nevertheless, the ceremonial laws relative to those suffering from this plague may be used to illustrate the effect of sin upon one's relation to God and to his fellow men.

To the treatment of this subject Leviticus devotes

two chapters, one to the diagnosis of leprosy (Ch. 13), and one to its cleansing (Ch. 14).

Even the minute specifications for the detection of the disease do not determine its exact character. The term seems to have been applied to a variety of maladies and even to mildew and mold on garments and houses. The diagnosis was left to the priest, and the law seems to have had in view some very definite and dreadful form of the disease. It was subject to the most stringent regulations and its disappearance or cure was attended by the most elaborate ritual. In case of any suspicious affection of the skin, such as a swelling, a "bright spot" in which the hair turned white, or the appearance of "raw flesh," the sufferer must present himself to the priest. After examination, in case of doubt, he was segregated for seven days, or, if necessary, for fourteen days. "If the plague be somewhat dark, and the plague spread not in the skin, the priest shall pronounce him clean . . . but if the scab spread much abroad in the skin . . . then the priest shall pronounce him unclean: it is a leprosy." The fate of the leper was pitiful in the extreme. With rent clothing and disheveled hair, he was excluded from the congregation and driven from the camp. His upper lip was covered to prevent speech, but as anyone approached him he was to cry, "Unclean! Unclean!" lest he be touched. The rules he was to observe were those of mourning for the dead. He was to regard himself as dead and others were so to regard him, so truly was he cut off from the life of the people.

These severe, even harsh restrictions, were probably for sanitary reasons, designed to prevent contagion and the spread of disease. However, religious conceptions were involved. The leper was unclean not only physically but ceremonially. One so repulsive in appearance was regarded not as morally at fault but as bodily unfit to mingle with the worshipers of a holy God.

It is not at all surprising that such a malady has been regarded as a type of sin. It was supposed to be *hereditary*. Its attack was *insidious*, scarcely noticed at first, rapidly spreading, at times disappearing, to break out again in a more serious form. It was *progressive*, usually advancing relentlessly. It was *pervasive*, limited to no one part of the victim, but soon affecting the whole body until the sufferer was a living corpse. It was *benumbing*, as in some cases the parts affected ceased to be sensitive. It was *loathsome*. This was its most characteristic feature. It was *isolating*, shutting one off from the congregation of worshipers. All this is quite true of sin; but leprosy is no longer regarded as hereditary. Children of lepers, if they are taken from their parents and properly cared for, are free of the disease. Yet, in a general way, the analogy will hold, and the comparison is calculated to make one shudder at the most dreadful of all maladies, namely, the moral evil which threatens to pervade one's whole being and which separates one from his fellows and from his God.

There surely is a cure for sin, and with the analogy still in mind, it is a relief to turn to the ordinance which deals with the *cleansing of leprosy* (Ch. 14).

While commonly regarded as incurable, it is clear that the disease described in the Bible ran its course, in certain cases, or was arrested by the direct power of God. This is evident from the fact that an elaborate ritual was established for the purification of the leper and for his restoration to his home and to the fellowship of worshipers. This ritual was divided into three stages: (1) a legal ceremony "outside the camp" by which the leper was readmitted to his civil status, (2) an act of personal, physical purification, and (3) a religious ceremony at the door of the tabernacle by which he was admitted again to full privileges as a worshiper of God.

1. The leper who believed that he had been cured of the plague went to an appointed place near the border of the camp. There he was met by the priest, who must attest the cure. Two living birds were provided, also a bunch of hyssop, tied by a band of scarlet wool to a rod of cedar. One of the birds was killed and its blood allowed to fall into a vessel containing water from a spring or from a flowing stream. The living bird and the hyssop were then dipped into a vessel and with the mingled water and blood the leper was sprinkled seven times and pronounced clean; then the living bird was let loose "into the open field."

Just what each detail of this ceremony meant to the ancient Israelites is not quite certain, nor can one affirm positively what it is intended to teach the people of God today. However, there can be no doubt that the water and blood symbolized cleansing, and apparently the release of the living bird, which had been dipped in the water and blood, indicated the complete removal of all uncleanness. Many readers see in this release the complete deliverance of the leper from his former condition. According to the ritual (vs. 52, 53), both the sprinkling and the release were regarded as an "atonement." The restoration to a place among the covenant people of God had been secured.

It has been natural for Christians to find in this ritual a type of the cleansing effected by "the water and the blood," the "double cure." It is supposed to picture the work of the Saviour who came "not by water only but by water and blood" (I John 5:6). Many find in this ritual the real meaning of the Psalmist in his penitential plea, "Purge me with hyssop, and I shall be clean; wash me, and I shall be whiter than snow" (Psalm 51:7).

2. There was something, however, which a leper must do for himself before he could be restored to his home or to his place as a worshiper. He must purify himself. The ritual of purification was performed twice. The clothing had to be washed, the body bathed, the hair shaved. Then the sufferer could enter the camp, but after seven days this cleansing had to be repeated, even more carefully. The very eyebrows had to be shaved. Every possible precaution was taken that no sign of leprosy, no possibility of its taint, be brought into the home of the cleansed leper or into the company of the covenant people. By way of analogy, it is true that one who has been sprinkled and made clean by the blood of Christ, one who is to enjoy the fellowship of Christians, must feel an absolute obligation resting on him to have and maintain purity of character and life, to "keep himself unspotted from the world."

3. On the eighth day the supreme portion of the ritual was enacted. The cleansed leper was restored to all the privileges of worship and of fellowship with God. He was brought to the door of the tabernacle. He presented three offerings, a lamb for a trespass (or "guilt") offering, another for a sin offering, a ewe lamb for a burnt offering, and three "meal offerings" of flour and oil, one for each of the animal sacrifices.

These offerings had their usual significance as previously set forth (Chs. 1-7) and, as here declared, they made "atonement" for the cleansed leper. They brought him into renewed fellowship with God. However, the ritual of the trespass offering is unique and significant. The entire offering, and also the oil of the meal offering were "waved before the Lord," that is, they were presented and then returned to the worshiper. The flesh belonged to the priest and the blood was applied to the cleansed leper. The ritual, surprising enough, was the same -as that prescribed for the consecration of priests. There is this difference, however: in consecrating the priest the blood employed was that of the peace offering; in cleansing the leper, it was that of the trespass offering. The reason for the prominence given to the trespass or guilt offering in this ritual was its peculiar significance. The trespass offering was the sacrifice designed to render satisfaction for any injury done to another, and also for failing to perform any due service. By his uncleanness, the leper had been prevented from rendering to God the sacrifice and service of a true worshiper; now by his trespass offering he made reparation for the failure and loss.

The importance of this trespass offering was further emphasized by the fact that no matter how poor a restored leper might be, he must present a lamb, while for a sin offering or a burnt offering he might substitute turtle doves or pigeons.

The blood of this trespass offering was applied as in the consecration of priests, to an ear, a hand and a foot of the cleansed leper. Expiation thus was made for any previous wrong use of ear or hand or foot, and these were now dedicated as instruments for the service of God. After this there was a similar application of oil to the meal offering, and oil was poured on the head of the worshiper, symbolizing his complete dedication to the Lord. Thus cleansed with blood and consecrated with the oil, the healed leper was restored to fellowship with the people of God and to all the privileges of true worship.

The statement of the laws for discerning leprosy in a man or a woman was followed by regulations concerning the *leprosy of a garment* (Ch. 13), and after the ritual for the cleansing of the leper there was added a paragraph relating to *leprosy in a house* (Ch. 14). Was this leprosy of clothing and buildings merely mildew or mold or vegetable fungus, or was it the work of bacteria, or vegetable parasites causing a condition which could be regarded as actual leprosy? Whichever view is taken, evidently in all cases there was need of purification both physical and ceremonial. If a leprous spot appeared on a garment, the garment had to be washed. If, after seven days, examination showed that the spot was still present or was spreading, the garment had to be burned. If a house was involved, the stones showing signs of the plague had to be removed and the plaster scraped from the walls. If the plague reappeared, the house had to be destroyed and the materials carried outside the city. If, however, the spot should not reappear, the house was to be declared clean, and the priest was to take two birds and cedar and scarlet and hyssop and enact the same ritual as in the purification of the leper.

It is evident that these regulations concerning garments and houses had in view preservation of property and protection of health. Yet the sprinkling with water and blood and the whole ceremonial, so precisely like that of cleansing the leper or consecrating the priests, indicated that to the ancient Israelite the regulations must have had not only sanitary but also religious implications. The holy God required the very garments and homes of His people to be holy. This is emphasized in the closing paragraph of the ritual: "He shall let go the living bird out of the city into the open fields, and make an atonement for the house, and it shall be clean" (Ch. 14:53). In all ages it is required of a true worshiper that he should be pure and holy in his habits and surroundings. The very home of a Christian should be a house of God.

The Cleansing of Bodily Issues. [Ch. 15]

Bodily issues were not regarded as sinful, but they did require ceremonial purification. These ceremonies had a definite meaning. The issues specified were all concerned with the processes of reproduction. The necessity of their cleansing was an implication that the very sources of life have been affected by sin. As members of the human race our very being and states as well as our acts are imperfect and need divine purifying if we are to have fellowship with a holy God.

The first part of the chapter relates to the purification of men (vs. 2-18); the second, to the purification of women (vs. 19-30). In either case a natural issue must be cleansed by bathing and a person must be regarded as "unclean until evening." Abnormal issues were more serious and required a special ceremonial of cleansing. While the issue continued, everything or person touched was made unclean. When the issue had stopped, seven days must pass; then, on the eighth day, the affected person must come before the priest and present a burnt offering and a sin offering, with which an "atonement" was made "before the Lord." No doubt the first reason for these requirements was sanitary and had regard for the preservation of health. Another purpose was the maintenance of moral purity. And besides the physical and moral implications, there was a religious aim. The ceremony indicated that whatever our moral and spiritual infirmity may be, an atoning sacrifice and a cleansing by the Holy Spirit is required if we are to be restored to fellowship with God. The solemn message is embodied in a paragraph with which the ritual closes: "Thus shall ye separate the children of Israel from their uncleanness; that they die not in their uncleanness, when they defile my tabernacle that is among them" (v. 29).

The pain of death attached to one who attempted to worship before being made clean. We can have confidence in the promise, "If we confess our sins, he is faithful and just to forgive us our sins, and to cleanse us from all unrighteousness" (I John 1:9). This ritual makes more impressive the miracle performed by our Lord. A poor woman who for twelve years had suffered from her affliction "came behind him, and touched the hem of his garment: for she said within herself, If I may but touch his garment, I shall be whole." Full well did she know that, according to the law, her touch would be defiling; but she believed His divine power would neutralize any uncleanness and would heal her disease. "But Jesus turned him about, and when he saw her, he said, Daughter, be of good comfort; thy faith hath made thee whole" (Matthew 9:20-22).

THE DAY OF ATONEMENT. [Ch. 16]

The *supreme chapter* of the Book of Leviticus is the sixteenth. It is, in fact, the climax of the whole Mosaic sacrificial system. Provision had been made for the forgiveness of individuals, but here is a service in which is symbolized atonement for all the sins of a nation. Then, too, atonement is made, not only for the people but for the priests, and for the tabernacle and for the sacred altars. It indicated the imperfection, even the sinfulness, of the most holy acts and services. Day by day, sins had been confessed and sacrifices had been offered, but now, once a year, on this day of days, expiation is made for "all the iniquities of the children of Israel, and all their transgressions, even all their sins."

This is a gratifying chapter to all who attempt to interpret the Old Testament types and symbols, for in this interpretation there always is the danger of indulging one's fancy and of finding analogies and meanings for which there is no Scriptural warrant. However, for the ritual of the Day of Atonement there is a detailed explanation in the Epistle to the Hebrews. The very heart of that inspired letter deals with the atoning work of Christ, our Great High Priest; and in its climactic ninth chapter all the figures and symbols are drawn from the ritual recorded in this sixteenth chapter of Leviticus; and, strange to say, reference to this ritual is found in no other place in the Old Testament.

This is a very *significant chapter*. It makes clear the real meaning of the atoning work of Christ, of His appearing as man, of His sacrificial death, of His entrance into the heavenly sanctuary, of His present intercession and of His coming glory. Here, indeed, we have in symbol the whole story of redemption. Thus this ritual is the Gospel according to Moses.

The central figure in the ceremonies of the Day of Atonement was that of the High Priest. He alone, and only on that day, could enter the Holy of Holies. Yet all the people expressed their vital interest and concern. They rested from all manner of work, and "they afflicted their souls" by observing a solemn fast as they expressed their repentance and their sorrow for sin. Thus, while, as Christians, we have no part in the atoning work of Christ, that atonement avails for us only in case of true repentance and of sympathetic trust.

The high priest needed to prepare himself for the solemn services of the day. He put off his resplendent robes "for glory and beauty," and when he had bathed his body with water, he clothed himself with a white garment similar to that which was worn by the other members of his household. This white linen thus was not merely a symbol of purity, but likewise of humility. One remembers how our Great High Priest, for our redemption, laid aside the "form of God" . . . and "took upon him the form of a servant . . . and humbled himself and became obedient unto death" (Philippians 2:6-8). Yet He was sinless. He was typified by the high priest, who was clothed in white and also had inscribed on the golden crown of his white turban, "Holiness to Jehovah."

The *sacrifices* presented by the high priest on the Day of Atonement were a bullock, as a sin offering for himself and his family; two goats, as a sin offering for the people; and a ram, as a burnt offering for himself, and another for the "congregation."

First of all, the high priest sacrifices the sin offering for himself to make an atonement for himself and for his house. His own sins needed to be expiated before he could offer sacrifices for the people. In the Epistle to the Hebrews this fact is contrasted with the atoning work of Christ: "Such an high priest became us, who is holy, harmless, undefiled, separate from sinners . . . who needeth not . . . to offer sacrifices, first for his own sins, and then for the people's" (Hebrews 7:26, 27). This whole system of symbols was superseded by the ministry of Christ, in whom the types found their fulfilment.

After offering the bullock as his sin offering, Aaron, the high priest, makes his entrance into the Holy of Holies. He holds a censer full of live coals from the altar of sacrifice, and carries with him a quantity of incense. He pours this on the coals, and the cloud which arises and fills the sacred shrine makes a veil between the presence of God and the priest, who even in an act of worship could not "see God and live" (Exodus 33:20).

A second time he enters the Holy of Holies, this time with the blood of his sin offering. This blood is sprinkled "with his finger upon the mercy seat eastward," that is, toward God. This was for the expiation of his own sins and the sins of his house. The blood was sprinkled "seven times before the mercy seat," that is, on the floor of the sanctuary, to symbolize the cleaning of this holiest place. Even such a sanctuary had become unclean because it had been surrounded by a sinful people. This sprinkling of the blood was the peculiar feature of the ritual, and such a use of this blood of the sin offering was made on this day alone. Thus it appears that when the New Testament speaks of "the sprinkling of blood" the reference is not to the Levitical sacrifices in general, but to this particular sin offering on the Day of Atonement (Hebrews 12:24; I Peter 1:2).

The sin offering for the people consisted of two "he-goats." Lots were cast and one of these two was set aside to be slain. With the blood of this sacrifice Aaron enters into the Holy of Holies a third time. He repeats the same ceremony now, not for himself, but for all the people, sprinkling the mercy seat and the Holy of Holies to make atonement "because of the uncleanness of the children of Israel, and because of their transgressions in all their sins" (v. 16).

Furthermore, as he returned he cleansed the court of the tabernacle by sprinkling the blood, and he purified the brazen altar by placing blood on its horns. Then followed the most peculiar and most unique feature of the ceremonial appointed for the Day of Atonement. It concerned the second of the two goats which together had been appointed "for a sin offering for the congregation." The service is thus described: "And when he had made an end of reconciling the holy place, and the tabernacle of the congregation, and the altar, he shall bring the live goat: and Aaron shall lay both his hands upon the head of the live goat, and confess over him all the iniquities of the children of Israel, and all their transgressions in all their sins, putting them upon the head of the goat, and shall send him away by the hand of a fit man into the wilderness: and the goat shall bear upon him all their iniquities unto a land not inhabited: and he shall let go the goat in the wilderness" (vs. 20-22).

A more vivid symbol of atonement can hardly be conceived. When Aaron lays both his hands on the head of the goat and confesses over him "all the iniquities of the children of Israel," substitution and imputation seem to be perfectly expressed. We think at once of the vicarious sufferer: "Surely he hath borne our griefs and carried our sorrows . . . and the Lord hath laid on him the iniquity of us all" (Isaiah 53:4, 6).

When the "scapegoat" bears away the transgressions of the people to a "land not inhabited" and is "let go in the wilderness," we have a vivid picture of the complete removal of sin. We hear the music of the Psalmist, "As

far as the east is from the west, so far hath he removed
our transgressions from us" (Psalm 103:12).

The meaning of this ritual appears quite clear. However, it contains one word which has occasioned endless
controversy. It is the word rendered as "scapegoat," literally "Azazel." Many insist that this is a proper name
which designated an evil spirit supposed to dwell in the
wilderness, and to whom the sins of the people were
sent. The familiar word "scapegoat" conveys a more popular meaning. It is not a translation but a statement of
the use for which the goat was designated. The margin
of the Revised Version translates the word as "removal"
or "dismissal." This part of the sin offering was to bear
away to a solitary place all the iniquities of the children
of Israel, which symbolically had been placed upon him.

As the sacrifice of the first goat signified the *means*
of reconciliation with God, namely, by the death and the
sprinkled blood of a vicarious offering, so the dismissal of
the second goat typified the *effect* of the expiation in the
removal of the sin from the presence of the holy God.
Together these two features of the sin offering indicate
the full meaning of atonement. It is significant that such
prominence is given to this offering in the annual ceremony established to indicate atonement made for the
people of Israel. Atonement is the word uniformly employed in the ritual of the sin offering. Atonement was
the aim and purpose of this offering. As has been said,
"to atone means to cover sin before God," that is, to
deprive it of its power to come between us and God. The
ceremonies of this annual observance, and particularly
the ritual of the sin offering, indicated that a sinful
people were pardoned and cleansed and restored to full
communion as worshipers of God.

When Aaron had performed the ceremony connected with the scapegoat, he once again entered the tabernacle. He removed his garments of white linen, and when he had again bathed, he assumed his imposing robes "for beauty and glory" and came forth to sacrifice the burnt offering for himself and the people "in token of complete reconsecration to the service of God." Then the bodies of the sin offerings were taken outside the camp and consumed by fire.

Thus when one has accepted anew the truth concerning the atoning work of Christ, he naturally desires to consecrate himself wholly to the service of his Saviour and his Lord.

In making his unique use of the ritual of the Day of Atonement the author of the Epistle to the Hebrews dwells in particular on two of its main features, the shedding of blood and the entrance into the Holy of Holies: "But Christ being come an high priest of good things to come, by a greater and more perfect tabernacle, not made with hands, . . . neither by the blood of goats and calves, but by his own blood he entered in once into the holy place, . . . into heaven itself, now to appear in the presence of God for us" (Hebrews 9:11, 12, 24). "Wherefore he is able also to save them to the uttermost that come unto God by him, seeing he ever liveth to make intercession for them" (Hebrews 7:25).

As when the atoning ritual had been fulfilled, when the blood had been sprinkled, when the ceremony within the veil had ended, Aaron, arrayed in his glorious garments, came forth from the tabernacle and again appeared to the expectant people, "so Christ also having been offered to bear the sins of many shall appear a

second time apart from sin, to them that wait for him,
unto salvation" (Hebrews 9:28 R.V.).

SEPARATION. *Moral Holiness.* [Chs. 17 to 22]

In the ritual for the Great Day of Atonement the
Book of Leviticus reached its climax. Laws had been
given concerning priesthood and ceremonial purification.
The culminating place in this ritual provided for that
great day of national cleansing (Chs. 1-16). The section
which follows is known as the "Law of Holiness" (Chs.
17-26). It relates to moral purity and to those regulations
which would keep the people free from uncleanness and
from the immoral practices of other nations. This was
designed to make Israel a blessing to the whole world by
its holiness and its witness to a holy God.

The "Law of Holiness" appears in two sections: Separation and Moral Holiness (Chs. 17-22), Holy Seasons
or the Times for Worship (Chs. 23-26).

HOLINESS IN EATING. [Ch. 17]

The statement that the opening chapters of the law
of holiness concern moral rather than ceremonial purity
seems to be contradicted by the ordinances concerning
the killing of animals intended for food. These regulations involved a very definite ritual. However, they did
not repeat the laws concerning clean and unclean animals,
nor did they relate to the ceremonial cleanness of worshipers. They were designed to preserve the moral purity
of the people by keeping them free from the practices of
idolatrous nations. The regulations were as follows, and
to them was added a statement of their definite purpose:

When an animal fit for sacrifice was to be used for food, "an ox, or lamb, or goat," it was to be brought to the priest at the door of the tabernacle and offered as a "peace offering unto the Lord." The blood caught in a bowl by the priest was to be sprinkled on the ground or poured upon the walls of the altar of burnt offering. The fat was to be burned for a "sweet savour unto the Lord." When the priest had taken his allotted portion of the flesh, the remainder was returned to the one who had presented the offering. It was to be regarded as a gift from God.

Surely all this was ceremonial, but the moral intent was stated at once: "To the end that the children of Israel may bring their sacrifices unto the Lord . . . and they shall no more offer their sacrifices unto devils, after whom they have gone a whoring." The surrounding nations connected idolatrous practices with the killing of their animals for food. These practices were usually grossly immoral. The law of Moses would keep the Israelites from the idolatry by which they were surrounded and remind them of their relation to God. Their very food was to be held sacred. It was to be offered to the Lord and accepted again as a bounty from him (vs. 1-7).

It may be questioned whether it would be possible for such a ritual to be observed, involving as it did the food of so great a multitude of people. Could every animal intended for food be brought to the door of the tabernacle and be treated by the priest as a peace offering? By way of reply, it may be recalled that little meat could be obtained or was used as food by the Israelites while they were in the wilderness. Furthermore, the tribes were closely gathered within the camp. When

Canaan had been reached and food was more abundant and the people were widely scattered, this law was repealed (Deuteronomy 12:15, 16, 20-24). Even while this ritual was in force it applied only to a few animals, to oxen, sheep and goats, and even these were to be of a certain age and particularly qualified as offerings. These too were treated as symbols and represented all the provisions granted by God to sustain the life of His people.

The ceremony which represented these animals as a peace offering was a true recognition of the fact that "every good and perfect gift" is from God. Our custom of returning thanks for daily food has the same meaning and may secure the same moral results. It invests our meals with a certain dignity and guards our social gatherings against intemperance and impropriety. It seems to have been a practice of the early Christians. When Paul rebukes the ascetic prohibition of certain kinds of food, he insists that "every creature of God is good, and nothing to be refused, if it be received with thanksgiving: for it is sanctified by the word of God and prayer" (I Timothy 4:4, 5).

The ordinance concerning the killing of animals for food had referred to these animals as "sacrifices," since they were to be treated as peace offerings. They were to be presented "at the door of the tabernacle" (vs. 1-7). Quite logically, there followed the regulation that every "burnt offering or sacrifice" of any kind, whether presented by an Israelite or by a foreigner residing among the people, must likewise be offered at the "door of the tabernacle of the congregation," and in no other place. To this regulation was given the most solemn sanction. Any man disobeying it would be "cut off from among the people." The purpose of this law was to give unity to the national life, but also to preclude all possibility of partaking in idolatrous practices. All sacrifices were to be offered at one sacred place and with the aid of an ordained priest. The worshiper could have in mind no strange deity, but would realize that he was in the presence of the one living and true God (vs. 8, 9).

Then followed a most strict and explicit prohibition against the *eating of blood*. This already had been secured by the ordinances relating to sacrifices. Specific instruction had been given for the disposition of the blood which was to be sprinkled or poured out. However, there were many "clean" animals which could be eaten as food besides those properly offered in sacrifice, particularly those taken in hunting. These might be killed at a great distance from the tabernacle. There might be a temptation to use the blood for food. Explicit directions, therefore, were given. The blood must be poured out and covered with earth.

So, too, with an animal which died a natural death or which had been torn by wild beasts—it could not be eaten, for a portion of the blood had been retained. One who ate such blood unwittingly would be defiled. He must "both wash his clothes, and bathe himself in water, and be unclean until the even." No blood could be eaten. This in itself would make an impressive distinction from the customs of heathen nations. Furthermore, it would be a safeguard against disease, for it is in the blood that the germs of infection circulate. Yet, aside from these reasons, the prohibition was explained by the specific text of the law. The statement is very striking, both from a scientific and a religious point of view. "For the life of the flesh is in the blood: and I have given it to you upon the altar to make an atonement for your souls: for it is the blood that maketh an atonement for the soul" (v. 11). *"The life of the flesh is in the blood."* Only in modern days has the full meaning of these words been realized. Blood is known to be the vital principle of the physical body. The discovery of the circulation of the blood was revolutionary in the study of anatomy. In more recent years it has been demonstrated that the health of the body depends on the rapidity of the blood flow; and blood transfusions are an accepted means of prolonging life.

However, the use of blood for food was forbidden on religious grounds. First, as "the life is in the blood," it belongs to God. He has created life and it returns to Him. He would have His people understand that all life is sacred.

Second, it is the appointed means for the expiation of sin: "I have given it to you upon the altar to make an atonement for your souls." This statement points back to the Day of Atonement and to all the ceremonial regulations which precede it. It is the only explanation given as to the meaning of these regulations. Until this passage, the meaning of the shedding of blood seems to have been taken for granted. Here the spiritual meaning of the symbols is set forth. The life of a substitute must be given to make atonement; and "without shedding of blood there is no remission of sins."

Still more eloquently does this passage point us forward to the statements of the New Testament and its marvelous mysterious revelation of the atoning work of Christ. We understand something of the symbolism. It is not blood as a physical substance, but blood which is shed, a life poured out, which secures atonement.

It is also blood on the altar. It is life offered to God

in willing sacrifice, which has made atonement for our souls. "In burnt offerings and sacrifices for sin thou hast had no pleasure. Then said I, Lo, I come to do thy will, O God. . . . By the which will we are sanctified through the offering of the body of Jesus Christ once for all" (Hebrews 10:6, 7, 9, 10). Thus it is by "the blood of Jesus" that we have "boldness to enter into the holiest." So this chapter in the ancient ritual of Leviticus enables us more fully to appreciate the atoning work of our Lord, and to fathom more deeply the profound meaning of these familiar messages: "We have redemption through his blood, even the forgiveness of sins" (Colossians 1:14); "The blood of Jesus Christ his Son cleanseth us from all sin" (I John 1:7); "They washed their robes, and made them white in the blood of the Lamb" (Revelation 7:14).

CHASTITY. [Ch. 18]

The three following chapters (18, 19, 20) form a distinct section in the "Law of Holiness." It is marked by a formal preface (Ch. 18:1-5) and a solemn conclusion (Ch. 20:22-26). It concerns not ceremonial but moral purity. Of the three chapters, the first and second contain prohibitions and precepts. The third states the penalties by which the laws were to be enforced. They all emphasize the fact that those who would worship God and have fellowship with Him not only must accept the means of approach which He has provided, but must be morally clean.

The eighteenth chapter deals with *laws of chastity*. The preface affirms the changeless standard of morality. This is found in the revealed will of God and is recorded in His word. Amid the terrors of Sinai the Israelites had made a covenant with God and had promised to keep His laws. They were required to avoid any practices, however prevalent, which were inconsistent with His commandments. The customs of the Egyptians among whom they had lived and the more gross immorality of the Canaanites were to be regarded with abhorrence. Looking backward to the moral corruption with which they had been familiar, and looking forward to the foul offenses by which they would be appalled, they were to remember the supremacy, the holiness, the perfect requirements and the certain punishments of their God. Obedience to His commandments would result in a life of true happiness and prosperity and peace. Such was the divine message: "After the doings of the land of Egypt, wherein ye dwelt, shall ye not do: and after the doings of the land of Canaan, whither I bring you, shall ye not do, neither shall ye walk in their ordinances. Ye shall do my judgments, and keep my ordinances to walk therein: I am the Lord your God. Ye shall therefore keep my statutes, and my judgments: which if a man do, he shall live in them: I am the Lord" (Ch. 18:3-5).

The people of God ever have been tempted to accept as standards of morality the practices of the society to which they belong, particularly when these practices are protected by law. The gross offenses against chastity prohibited in this chapter were not only "the doings of the land of Canaan," but, in many cases, they were actually "ordinances." They were legalized immoralities. The only right course is to remember the one supreme lawgiver: "Thou shalt worship the Lord thy God, and him only shalt thou serve."

The first of the prohibitions divinely imparted to Moses for the guidance of the children of Israel, as here recorded, related to the *degrees* of *kinship* forbidden in marriage. To us, such possible relationships seem shocking; but it must be remembered that among the surrounding nations, in the days of Moses, they were horribly prevalent.

The underlying principle, stated generally, forbids marriage with "any that is near of kin" (v. 6). Certain unlawful relationships are then specified. Incredible as these iniquities may seem, they were common among the Egyptians and the Canaanites. The criminal alliance of a man with his mother (v. 7) or his stepmother (v. 9) was a notorious infamy among the Medes and Persians. It was this which Paul severely rebuked when addressing the Corinthian Church, declaring that in his day it was not practiced even among the Gentiles (I Corinthians 5:1).

An unlawful union with a sister or half-sister needed to be specified. Abraham had married his half-sister, and marriage with full sisters was sanctioned by Egyptians and Assyrians and other nations of antiquity.

To marry a daughter or granddaughter was strictly forbidden; so was marriage with an aunt, although the latter was allowed by the Israelites at an earlier date. Such was the case of Amram and Jochebed, the ancestors of Moses and Aaron and Miriam. A man was not to marry the widow of his brother (v. 16). Yet this law was not absolute. In fact, when one died childless, it was the duty of his brother to marry the woman who had been his "brother's wife." If this second brother died, it was the duty of each surviving brother in turn to marry the widow and to raise up seed unto his brother. This was the law of the socalled "Levirate Marriage." It will be remembered that reference to this law was made by the

Sadducees in their effort to disprove the truth of the resurrection (Matthew 22:23-33).

Is it wrong to marry a deceased wife's sister? Those who have so contended have based their opinion on the prohibition: "Neither shalt thou take a wife to her sister, to vex her" (v. 18). This, however, was merely a restriction on polygamy. As in verse 17, it forbade a certain kind of polygamy, namely, the marriage with two sisters. The law specifically states, "Neither shalt thou take a wife to her sister . . . in *her life time*." This surely would seem to imply that after the death of a first wife a man could marry his sister-in-law. Moses did not forbid polygamy. He taught principles which ultimately would lead to the abolition of this iniquity. Yet, as in the case of divorce, he did all for the Israelites that "the hardness of their hearts" would allow. He insisted on regulations and restrictions which did much toward limiting the worst abuses of an evil institution (Matthew 19:3-12). So in this case, while not prohibiting polygamy, he strictly forbade one of its most odious and distressing forms, namely, taking as a rival wife the sister of one already married. This could only result in jealousy, and the natural love of sisters would be turned to bitter hatred. A situation would be created like that which Leah and Rachel, as wives of Jacob, were compelled to endure (v. 18).

It is best, therefore, to understand that this debated verse is a restriction on polygamy, as the next verse is on marriage relations (v. 19).

After a definite repetition of the Seventh Commandment, there follows the prohibition of one of the most horrible of heathen practices: "Thou shalt not let any of thy seed pass through the fire to Molech." This sacrificing of children as burnt offerings to a heathen god was allied to the other "abominations" here mentioned as reasons why God was to cast out of Canaan the people whose practices had defiled the land. The Israelites were warned that in spite of their covenant privileges they too would be driven out if they followed the vile customs for which the Canaanites justly were to be destroyed.

The mention of Molech, when this list of crimes is reaching its climax, reminds us of the inseparable connection between idolatry and immorality. In fact, these iniquities were prescribed forms of heathen worship. Paganism is inseparable from impurity, whether it is a paganism of the past or the refined paganism of the present day. Some of these forbidden practices are discovered even in Christian communities.

The closing paragraph of this chapter contains a solemn warning. Low standards of morals threaten the life of a nation, and even when a community as a whole may not be corrupt, every guilty individual offender will incur the penalties of divine displeasure. The purpose in all these Mosaic laws was the preservation of physical health, the protection of society, and the maintenance of spiritual life. The injunctions were based on the character of God. Worshipers in fellowship with Him must be holy as He is holy. Five times in this one chapter the solemn affirmation is repeated, "I am the Lord."

Precepts and Prohibitions. [Ch. 19]

In continuing the commands which belong to the "Law of Holiness" the conduct required is based on the same foundation, namely, the nature of God: "Ye shall be holy: for I the Lord your God am holy" (Ch. 19:2). However, the precepts which follow, while they relate in part to iniquities already mentioned, also reveal not only the justice of God, but His mercy and compassion and His care. They re-echo the words of the Ten Commandments recently pronounced at Sinai, but with additions indicating divine tenderness and love.

The opening division of these precepts (vs. 3-8) covers the ground, in general, of the first table of the Decalogue, "Thou shalt love the Lord thy God." The second division (vs. 9-18) corresponds to the second table of the Decalogue, "Thou shalt love thy neighbor as thyself."

The very first place is given to the Fifth Commandment, possibly because the honoring of parents is of such vital importance in the life of society, and because one usually learns to know God by a right relation to those who in a sense stand in the place of God.

Reverence for God is enjoined by three precepts: the keeping of Sabbaths, which acknowledges God's right to our time; refraining from idolatry in recognition of the divine claim, "I am the Lord your God," and careful observance of the law of the "peace offering." As to that offering, it was the sacrifice most frequently presented. A part belonged to the worshiper, who might be tempted to appropriate more than his portion instead of recognizing God by placing on the altar the whole portion which belonged to the Lord.

As to the precepts related in the second table of the law, the first group concerned care for the poor, "And when ye reap the harvest of your land, thou shalt not wholly reap the corners of thy field, neither shalt thou gather the gleanings of thy harvest. And thou shalt not glean thy vineyard, neither shalt thou gather every grape of thy vineyard; thou shalt leave them for the poor and stranger: I am the Lord your God" (vs. 9, 10).

By the first clause of this injunction we are transported in memory to the field of Boaz at Bethlehem. Because of her poverty, the young widow Ruth has gone out to glean at the time of harvest. With exquisite courtesy, her rich kinsman is saying to the reapers: "Let her glean even among the sheaves, and reproach her not: and let fall also some of the handfuls of purpose for her, and leave them, that she may glean them, and rebuke her not" (Ruth 2:16). He wished to help her, but he would not trespass on her independence. He also was obeying the command of "the Lord God of Israel under whose wings she had come to trust." Such consideration for the poor and the stranger revealed the character of God, not only in His majesty and purity, but also in His mercy and grace. Thus the familiar phrase is added, "I am the Lord your God."

The selfish greed which disregards the poor and grasps at the least handful of grain and the last cluster of grapes is closely related to the effort of securing something which rightfully belongs to our neighbor. Therefore, the next group of injunctions deals with theft and fraud. It refers to the eighth, the ninth, and the third commandments, but chiefly concerns stealing, which is as truly sinful in the form of fraud as in that of robbery. One may break the commandment by retaining that which should be given to the poor quite as much as by violently despoiling the rich. "Ye shall not steal; neither shall ye deal falsely nor lie one to another, and ye shall not swear by my name falsely so that thou profane the name of thy God: I am the Lord" (vs. 11, 12 R.V.).

The relation of these forbidden courses illustrates the

familiar fact that one sin always leads to another. He who
steals and defrauds will find it necessary to lie in order to
cover his iniquity. When the lie is questioned he will
swear falsely in the name of God and thus sin again by
profaning His holy name.

Injunctions against stealing and fraud naturally are
followed by warnings against oppression and heartless
cruelty, "Thou shalt not oppress thy neighbor nor rob
him; the wages of him that is hired shall not abide with
thee all night until the morning. Thou shalt not curse
the deaf, nor put a stumbling block before the blind, but
shalt fear thy God: I am the Lord" (vs. 13, 14).

Oppression may be cruel even when not violating
civil law. An employer may take an unfair advantage of
an employe; a creditor needlessly may distress an impov-
erished and poor debtor or cause his ruin by insisting on
the letter of a contract or the exact date of a promise.

So, too, a delay in the payment of wages may cause
a laborer embarrassment, anxiety, and distress. This practise of withholding the just reward of honest toil has been
common in all ages. The fault is severely rebuked in the
New Testament: "Behold, the hire of the laborers, who
have reaped down your fields, which is of you kept back
by fraud, crieth: and the cries of them which have reaped
are entered into the ears of the Lord of sabaoth" (James
5:4).

The cruel treatment of deaf or blind is a further example of the heartlessness which takes advantage of the
helpless. One may be irritated by the inability of the deaf
to understand what has been clearly stated and repeated;
yet it is unreasonable to expect the impossible, and unkind to find fault with those whose inability should arouse
only our sympathy. To speak harshly of those who can-

not defend themselves or reply to criticism or false statements is a grievous unkindness. Likewise, to place a stumbling block before the blind is a wanton cruelty. It is such an iniquity that it has been adopted in the moral and spiritual realm as an illustration of base treachery and betrayal.

The three preceding precepts have expressed sympathy for the poor, and the absolute necessity of preserving their rights. It was necessary, on the other hand, to insist on absolute justice to the rich as well as to the poor, specifically in the courts of law. It is to such legal procedures that the next precepts refer: "Thou shalt not go up and down as a talebearer among thy people: neither shalt thou stand against the blood of thy neighbor: I am the Lord. Thou shalt not hate thy brother in thy heart: thou shalt in any wise rebuke thy neighbor, and not suffer sin upon him" (vs. 15, 16).

These precepts need to be proclaimed in the present day. So much injustice has been done to the poor that many persons seem to feel that none is being done to the rich, and that the latter have no rights which anyone needs to respect. The cry for equality and for social security has made men deaf to the appeal for equal justice. The Communist theory that "capital is robbery" denies the right of private property. The confiscation of wealth has defied the law of God which declares, "Thou shalt not steal." To discourage industry, thrift, and enterprise, to so "respect the person of the poor" as to dishonor the "person of the mighty" is to disobey the command, "In righteousness shalt thou judge thy neighbor."

The justice required in courts of law, whether dealing with rich or poor, is often endangered by false testimony. To this reference is made by the phrase, "a talebearer among thy people." This should be rendered, "Thou shalt not go about slandering." Nor should one by such false testimony endanger the life of his neighbor. The supreme reason for justice to rich and poor is found in the presence of an unseen Judge whose decisions are infallible: "I am the Lord."

The series of precepts related to the conduct of man to man properly reach their climax in a group of precepts which enshrine the chief jewel of all moral laws: *"Thou shalt love thy neighbor as thyself."*

These precepts refer not only to outward acts, but to the mind and heart. Even when your neighbor has injured you no hatred should be harbored against him. It is your duty to reprove him for his wrong, otherwise you become a partaker of his offense and are guilty of secretly bearing ill will. While you are to rebuke, you are not to revenge. One even is to banish from memory any injury which has been done; he is to forgive and forget. This will be possible only as one loves his neighbor as he loves himself (vs. 17, 18).

The neighbor to whom, in the first instance, the precept applied was the fellow Israelite. The latter application was extended to "the stranger," that is, the foreigner dwelling among the people. It remained for Christ to give it universal and unlimited scope. He embodied His teaching in the immortal parable of the Good Samaritan (Luke 10:29-37), and in his answer to the question, "Which is the great commandment in the law?" (Matthew 22:36). Thus Paul also teaches that "love is the fulfilling of the law" (Romans 13:10).

The next division of the chapter (vs. 19-29) begins with a new call to obedience, possibly because the commands which follow may be regarded as less important

and therefore less likely to be obeyed. In fact, it is difficult to affirm the reason for some of these restrictions.
Some may have been symbolic and intended to teach
reverence for the divinely established order of nature.
Such may be the prohibition against raising hybrid animals, or sowing mixed seed, or wearing garments of
mingled linen and woolen (v. 19).

The law in reference to a guilty slave (vs. 20-22) may
seem to sanction slavery and its attendant evils. It was
not ideal, but as severe as the low moral tone of the community would have accepted. Slavery was an established
institution, and that law is best which will most effectively
restrain wrong conduct under existing conditions. This
ordinance, however, did recognize the slave as a person,
possessing sacred rights, and not as a mere chattel. In
time the principle stated and enforced by love for one's
neighbor led to the abolition of slavery as contrary to the
will of God.

The next precept (vs. 23-25) is one of the instances
which indicate that the laws of Leviticus were given to
the Israelites while they were in the wilderness and before
they reached the land of promise. (See 14:34; 19:23;
23:10; 25:2.) It provided that when they had "come into
the land" and had planted "all manner of trees for fruit,"
they should not eat of the fruit for the first three years.
They should regard it as "uncircumsized," that is, it had
not been presented unto the Lord and so was like a child
which had not been consecrated. In the fourth year,
when the fruit would be fully matured, it should be
offered to the Lord. The fruit of the fifth year could be
eaten by the people, who would be assured of the divine
blessing.

All this was in accordance with the law of "first

fruits." Therefore the fruit of the trees when fully ripe and matured belonged to the Lord. The people of God should always present to Him the first and best of all they enjoy. This recognizes Him as the "giver of every good and perfect gift," and implies that all we possess has come from Him to whom in our offerings we present tokens of our gratitude and devotion.

The four verses which follow (vs. 26-29) refer to heathen practises from which Israel as a holy nation must refrain. No blood was to be eaten, not only because of the ceremonial laws already enacted, but because this custom was connected with pagan rites. Charms and enchantments and divination from omens were prohibited. The hair or the beard was not to be cut in imitation of prevalent idolatrous practises, nor was sorrow for the dead to be expressed by cutting or disfiguring the body. The custom of tattooing was forbidden, while among all the nations of antiquity it was common; a slave carried the initials of his master, a soldier those of his general, the worshiper bore the image of his god. To avoid this disfiguring of the body the Hebrew wore his phylacteries as an emblem of his creed. These were a "sign" on the hand and a "memorial" between the eyes, indicating that the law of the Lord would be remembered and obeyed. The last provision (v. 29) refers to a horrible custom which formed a part of the degrading worship of Astarte. Surely a people which practised or permitted such crimes was certain to make "the land become full of wickedness."

The closing injunctions of the chapter (vs. 30-37) are prefaced by a command, obedience to which is a sure foundation for morality and a safeguard for social and national life: "Ye shall keep my sabbaths and reverence my sanctuary: I am the Lord" (v. 30). Observance of the Lord's day and attendance at the house of the Lord, even though perfunctory, do tend to keep in mind "the God of the sabbath and the God of the sanctuary," and the remembrance of God is sure to restrain immorality and is an incentive to holiness of life.

On the contrary, the people of God were not to inquire of those who had "familiar spirits," necromancers who profess to communicate with the dead, or with "wizards" who pretended to foretell the future and to make revelations by superhuman power. This is rather a precise description of the delusions which are being practised widely today. If such recourse to spirits was regarded as "defiling" by the ancient people of God, it is difficult to believe that such practises can be other than demoralizing to the followers of Christ.

While these soothsayers and spiritists are not to be respected, the aged are to be reverenced, as God also is to be held in holy regard: "Thou shalt rise up before the hoary head, and honor the face of the old man, and fear thy God: I am the Lord" (v. 32). It must be confessed that due respect for the aged often is more scrupulously shown by the adherents of Oriental religions than in Christian communities. At least, there is need of this serious injunction to give due regard to the aged and true reverence to God.

This command is closely related to the injunction to treat with kindness foreigners dwelling among the Israelites, "And if a stranger sojourn with thee, thou shalt not vex him" (v. 33). That is to say, thou shalt do no wrong to one who, although foreign born, has come to accept the religion and all the laws and customs of Israel. "Thou shalt love him as thyself." Not only is he to be treated with the courtesy and justice due to every fellow man, but to him is to be applied that "royal law" of love which here again is repeated. The Israelites should be the more inclined to such kindness toward strangers when they remembered how recently they themselves had been "strangers" in the land of Egypt (v. 34).

The last injunction of this law of holiness insists on absolute honesty in all commercial transactions: "Ye shall do no unrighteousness in judgment, in meteyard, in weight, or in measure" (v. 35). The phrase, "shall do no unrighteousness," is the same as in verse fifteen, in which it refers to a court of law. One who defrauds his neighbor in the use of meteyard (or measuring rod), or in the size of his "ephah" (a dry measure of about one bushel), or in the contents of a "hin" (a liquid measure of a gallon and a half), would be as truly a criminal as a judge who in a court of justice should wilfully pronounce a false sentence. "Just balances, just weights, a just ephah, and a just hin, shall ye have" (v. 36). That is, these measures were to be the same for buying as for selling. Fraud by means of false measures, whether by dishonest use of scales or by payments in depressed currency, has been common in all countries. The Israelites should be the more inclined to absolute honesty when they remember that they were a redeemed people. God had brought them "out of the land of Egypt." Therefore they should "observe" His statutes, and His "judgments, and do them" (vs. 37).

It is very evident that the holiness required by the Lord was much more than observance of the Sabbath and attendance on divine worship. It consisted quite as much in maintenance of absolute standards of conduct every day and in all the relations of life. The same motive to which Moses twice appeals in these closing verses (vs. 33, 36) may well be remembered by all the followers of Christ. They, too, form a redeemed people and should be holy because they have been "redeemed not with corruptible things as silver and gold . . . but with the precious blood of Christ" (I Peter 1:18, 19).

PENALTIES. [Ch. 20]

Shall capital punishment be abolished, and if so by what sanctions shall it be replaced? What purposes should be served in the treatment of criminals? What are the proper principles underlying a penal code? These difficult questions cannot be answered merely by quoting the laws of Leviticus; however, they should never be decided without reference to the legislation of Moses. The three chapters which, in part, record the "Law of Holiness" (Chs. 18, 19, 20) form only a portion of this legal code, and their provisions need to be read in the light of its other enactments. However, they form a unit and embody abiding principles. The eighteenth chapter names certain serious and revolting crimes. The twentieth chapter specifies the penalties by which these crimes should be punished. The nineteenth chapter records lesser faults and contains provisions for social justice and mercy. It twice records the supreme command found in no other chapter of the Old Testament, "Thou shalt love thy neighbor as thyself." Such requirements prepare one to read the solemn provisions of this twentieth chapter.

Here the death penalty is appointed for sacrificing children to the god Molech, for necromancy, for cursing parents, for adultery, for incest, for sodomy, and for bestiality, while lesser punishments are to be inflicted for

other crimes. All these offenses are to be punished on
the ground that they identify the people of God with
heathen nations, whereas they had been called to be separate from other people. This separation was to be
marked even by the distinction they made between different kinds of food. The reason divinely given was this:
"Ye shall be holy unto me, for I the Lord am holy."

This code has been criticized on the ground of its too
great severity. It is true that circumstances and conditions
change the character of legal sanctions. The Israelites
were a somewhat undisciplined race, recently released
from degrading bondage, and for them extreme punishments may have been necessary; yet in the very matter of
the death penalty this code of Moses was far more lenient
than those of other peoples. In fact, it was centuries in
advance of even the most cultivated and refined nations,
which inflicted the death penalty for a large number of
comparatively trivial offenses. This was true of England
until recent times. Now English law restricts the death
penalty to "high treason" and murder "with malice afore-
thought." Such restriction reminds one of these very
laws of Moses. Death was inflicted only for unnatural
and revolting crimes, and for those which could be regarded as treason and murder. The worship of Molech
(vs. 1-5) involved the cruel sacrifice of innocent children
burned by worshipers of the god. Wizards and necromancers were punished because their practises were closely
associated with the abominations of heathen religions (vs.
6, 27). The cursing of parents and the sins of impurity
were crimes which imperiled the very existence of the
family. They were not the murder of an individual but
the destruction of the sacred institution on which the
security of society was based.

If the Mosaic code is found to have been too severe, shall not our modern treatment of crime be regarded as too lenient? Of the "abominations" which, together with adultery, were punished by death, some are practised today among even Christian nations; but not one of them is subject to the death penalty. Most of them are unrecognized by the law. Some have what, practically, is legal sanction. This is particularly true of the present-day treatment of divorce. By many enactments the Seventh Commandment is annulled, and, in circles of culture, it is regarded as a dead letter. Much present-day sentimentality makes heroes of criminals and condones the most flagrant forms of social vice.

The reasons given for the infliction of severe penalties were twofold. First, the offenses in question were in open defiance of God and in disregard of His established laws. As God had been accepted as King of Israel such conduct was actual treason. Second, the penalties imposed had a view to the preservation of society. They were designed to keep Israel free from the immoralities inseparable from idolatry.

This purpose is emphasized as the chapter comes to its close. Indeed, the paragraph is an appropriate conclusion to the three chapters of this "Law of Holiness": "Ye shall therefore keep all my statutes, and all my judgments, and do them: that the land, whither I bring you to dwell therein, spue you not out. And ye shall not walk in the manners of the nation, which I cast out before you: for they committed all these things, and therefore I abhorred them. But I have said unto you, Ye shall inherit their land, and I will give it unto you to possess it, a land that floweth with milk and honey: I am the Lord your

God, which have separated you from other people" (vs. 22-24).

Such laws and such sanctions seemed necessary to preserve the life of the nation. They embody a solemn warning to the peoples of today Whether Canaanites or Israelites, no nation can, with impunity, deny the established laws of God. Only by obedience to these laws can peace and prosperity be assured. Most of all, to the followers of Christ comes the solemn injunction: "And ye shall be holy unto me: for I the Lord am holy, and have severed you from other people, that ye should be mine" (v. 26).

A review of the horrid list of revolting crimes which are named in these three chapters, and which have been committed in all ages of the world, is a humiliating demonstration of the truth that the heart of man is "deceitful above all things and desperately wicked." No terror of the law, no severity of punishment, ever has been able to restrain men from evil conduct. What the law failed to do, the Gospel promises to accomplish. "For what the law could not do, in that it was weak through the flesh, God sending his own Son in the likeness of sinful flesh, and for sin, condemned sin in the flesh; that the righteousness of the law might be fulfilled in us, who walk not after the flesh, but after the Spirit" (Romans 8:3, 4).

These pages from Leviticus emphasize the message of the Saviour, "Ye must be born again." Such spiritual rebirth is promised through faith in the Lord Jesus Christ. As men yield their lives to Him, in so far is there security for the family and the state.

Priestly Holiness. [Chs. 21 and 22]

There are not two standards of morality, one for the priest and another for the people, one for a minister and another for the members of his congregation, one for a Christian and another for a professed skeptic. The moral law as delivered at Sinai and recorded in the inspired word is infallible, universal, and unchanging. Yet high station and wide influence on the part of an offender makes disobedience to this law more serious and deserving of more severe penalties. It is also true that spiritual privileges and sacred duties involve larger responsibilities and demand greater perfection of character and conduct. Thus for the Israelites the statutes embodied in the "Law of Holiness" which were binding on all members of the community were followed by laws for the priests, who, by virtue of their sacred office, were to exhibit the highest degree of ceremonial and moral purity.

These laws are of obvious and immediate application to the followers of Christ, and particularly to those who occupy public positions as leaders and shepherds of the people of God. All believers form a royal priesthood. It is for them to serve for God with men. They are to represent God, to intercede for others and to offer spiritual sacrifices. Particularly is this true of those who are ordained to preach the Gospel, to administer sacraments, and to lead in the services of prayer and praise.

Because of their exalted privileges and special duties, there is expected of all such professing Christians and ordained ministers lives of unblemished virtue and unselfish service.

As the instructions on priestly holiness began, the

sons of Aaron were reminded that they were priests by
birth. Theirs was not a position which had been achieved
or one which they could abandon at will. However, they
might become guilty of conduct which would unfit them
for their sacred tasks. They must maintain not only moral
but ceremonial holiness. So it is with Christians. Their
position as priests is by virtue of a spiritual birth. They
owe their position to the grace of God. Yet their manner
of life, while not forfeiting the status of priests, may unfit
them for Christian service. It may mar or limit their
testimony for Christ.

1. The Hebrew priests were warned against ceremonial defilement resulting from *relations of friendship
and marriage*. They were not allowed to contract ceremonial uncleanness by coming into contact with the dead.
No claims of custom or respect would justify one in at-
tending the funeral rites of a friend or in making the
usual expressions of grief. Disobedience to this law might
involve no moral fault, but would render it impossible
for a priest to perform his sacred tasks. This requirement,
however, was to be applied with leniency, and would not
be enforced in the case of those who were near of kin.
Yet in the case of the high priest even this exception was
not made. Even the death of his father or mother could
not be an excuse for him to exhibit the usual signs of
mourning nor allow his service in the tabernacle to be
interrupted.

If contact with the dead could unfit one for priestly
service, much greater would be the danger from forbidden alliances with the living. A priest could marry only
a woman of unblemished reputation, not a divorced
woman whose husband was living; and the high priest
could not marry even a widow. Any immorality in the

family of a priest would be punished most severely. All his domestic relations should be holy. So it it with Christians, and particularly with ministers of the Gospel; social customs may be followed which, while not morally wrong, may be of such a character as to interfere with spiritual life and service. Particularly is it true that close friendships and, most of all, marriages with unbelievers, may imperil and retard religious experience and activity. Questionable companionships and intimacies must be avoided by all who hope to enjoy fellowship with Christ or to be helpful as children of God. "Wherefore come out from among them, and be ye separate, saith the Lord, and touch not the unclean thing; and I will receive you, and will be a Father unto you, and ye shall be my sons and daughters, saith the Lord Almighty" (II Corinthians 6:17, 18).

2. *Bodily blemishes* also disqualified the priest from active service: "Speak unto Aaron, saying, Whosoever he be of thy seed in their generations that hath any blemish, let him not approach to offer the bread of his God" (v. 17).

The priest might be a true son of Aaron, yet if blind, or lame, or disfigured, he could not have a part in the public service of the tabernacle; he could not pass within the "veil," nor "come nigh unto the Almighty" (v. 23). However, he enjoyed many privileges. He was supported by the offerings of the people. He was allowed to eat the bread of God, "both of the most holy, and the holy" (v. 22).

Is it not true that many Christians, even many in the sacred ministry, who enjoy spiritual privileges and experiences yet have such obvious moral defects as to debar them from success in the work for which otherwise they are well qualified? A hasty temper, a censorious spirit, avarice, jealousy, even spiritual pride, unfit for priestly service many who otherwise would be fruitful in the church. However, unlike certain physical defects, these moral infirmities can be removed in large measure by the power of our great High Priest. Indeed, one can grow into the likeness of Christ and be increasingly worthy of the exalted ministry to which he has been called as a priest of the Most High God (Ch. 21:16-24).

3. The priests, further, were encouraged to regard with reverence the *holy things* which were allotted as their portion. If ceremonially unclean they were not to eat of these offerings. "Whosoever he be of all your seed among your generation, that goeth unto the holy things, which the children of Israel hallow unto the Lord, having his uncleanness upon him, that soul shall be cut off from my presence: I am the Lord" (Ch. 22:3).

Such defilement might be due to contact with the dead or to a taint of leprosy or to partaking of some animal food which was regarded as unclean. Whatever the nature of the ceremonial uncleanness, it debarred a priest from partaking of the holy offerings.

Moreover, it was the duty of the priests to guard the holy things of the tabernacle by excluding from participation in these sacred portions of food all persons not belonging to the priestly order: "There shall no stranger eat of the holy thing: a sojourner of the priest, or an hired servant, shall not eat of the holy thing." However, if a slave had been purchased by the priest and became a member of the household, or if one was born in the home of a priest, he was allowed to eat this bread of God. "If the priest buy any soul with his money, he shall eat of it, and he that is born in his house: they shall eat of his meat" (v. 11). Even a daughter of a priest who had a family of her own was excluded; but if she returned to the priest's house, separated from her husband and childless, she could be admitted again to the sacred privileges belonging to the priestly order (vs. 12, 13).

These provisions have been cancelled in the letter, but they embody principles of abiding significance for the followers of Christ. First, as to reverence for holy things, there is ever the temptation to refer flippantly to the sacred Scriptures, to lack reverence for the house of God, and even to partake carelessly of the supper of our Lord. We must not judge ourselves too harshly, but is it not true that many partake of the sacrament thoughtlessly, carelessly, without truly examining themselves or seeking to discern the Lord's body, as Paul enjoined the Corinthians (I Corinthians 11:28, 29)? None of us is morally perfect. The holy supper is a place for confession and repentance and new resolution; but to accept the consecrated elements in fellowship with the followers of Christ, when conscious of sins which have not been confessed or abandoned, and without a definite dedication to the service of Christ, is a serious desecration of holy things.

Then, too, the priests were required to prevent "strangers" from eating the "bread of God." We must avoid unkind judgments or severe testing of candidates who desire to partake of the Holy Communion, but it is our duty as members of the Christian Church to see that real care is exercised as to the admission of "strangers" to the Table of our Lord. However, all persons should be welcomed who made a credible confession of their faith in Christ and who are willing to promise new obedience and devotion to Him.

4. In the fourth place, priestly holiness was required

in the matter of *sacrifices* which were to be presented to the Lord (vs. 11-37). These must not be worthless, nor must their offering involve cruelty: "Whatsoever hath a blemish, that shall ye not offer: for it shall not be acceptable for you" (v. 20). "Blind, or broken, or maimed, . . . ye shall not offer these" (v. 22). This prohibition also was extended to foreigners who desired to make an offering to the Lord.

Another restriction is added in this matter of sacrifices. It referred to the age of the offering. It must not be less than eight days old. Furthermore, a cow or a ewe could not be killed in the same day as her young. Evidently this was to prevent any appearance of heartlessness. Lastly, the flesh of a sacrifice must be eaten the same day on which it was offered. Probably this was to avoid any possibility of the flesh becoming tainted.

It is not difficult to apply practically to the conduct of Christians the principles involved in these prescriptions. Offerings which are to be presented to the Lord must be free from blemish. When judged by an absolute standard, none of our offerings is perfect. However, all must be the best we can provide. To offer to the Lord gifts which we know to be worthless and which are of no value to ourselves is impiety and sacrilege; but to offer what is precious to us and involves real self-denial, or serious effort, is an act of true worship; and, however imperfect such an offering may be, it will be received as a sacrifice and a "sweet odor" acceptable and well pleasing to the Lord.

Then, again, a sacrifice may involve unkindness or cruelty. A worshiper may contribute to religious objects so generously as to cause hardship and suffering to those who are dependent on him for support. An opposite peril is still more real and common, namely, for one to be so indulgent of his dependents as to make them selfish, extravagant, and indolent. The greatest legacy one can leave to his children is to teach them independence, frugality, industry, and thrift; and above all to train them in the Christian virtue of stewardship so that they can enjoy the great privilege of bringing to the altar of God sacrifices which will be well pleasing to Him.

III

THE TIMES FOR WORSHIP
LEVITICUS 23 to 26

A BOOK which is regarded as a Directory for Worship naturally contains a section relating to sacred times and seasons. Thus, when in Leviticus, *Provision for Worship* has been made in sacrifices and priesthood (Chs. 1-10) and when the *Requisite for Worship* has been set forth in ceremonial and moral holiness (Chs. 11-22), the last great section of the book concerns the *Times for Worship* (Chs. 23-26). As sacrifices symbolized "dedication," and priesthood, "meditation," and holiness, "separation," so these "times for worship" were symbols of "*consecration.*" Their observance was an indication on the part of the people that their time, their land, their harvests, their persons belonged to God.

It is true that these times were related to seasons of ingathering; but, unlike similar observances of other nations, these sacred observances were far more than harvest festivals. They were signs and seals of the covenant made with Jehovah. They did recognize God as the Author and Sustainer of life, but they reverenced Him as the Deliverer who had brought Israel out of bondage in Egypt, and at Sinai had given His law and had been acclaimed by the people as their King.

These sacred seasons, commonly are known as the "*Hebrew Feasts.*" Strictly speaking, only three of these "set times" were "feasts." The root of this word in Hebrew signifies "to dance." The term applies properly to seasons of special joy and thanksgiving and festivity. Such, indeed, were the feasts of Unleavened Bread, of Pentecost and of Tabernacles. Quite a different word is applied to the other sacred seasons, although it also is translated as "feasts." The Revised Version more accurately renders the term "set-feasts" or "appointed seasons," a term which was appropriate not only to the three "feasts" but to all the "set times of Jehovah."

These sacred "times for worship," formed a unique and symmetrical system. The formative factor was the sacred number seven. This number symbolized completeness and rest, whereas eight, the beginning of a new week, was a symbol of a new creation.

Thus the weekly Sabbath was the seventh day. This number seven also measured the length of the great feast of Unleavened Bread and the great feast of Tabernacles, which were seven days each. On the fourteenth day (two sevens) of the first month of the sacred year was celebrated the Feast of Passover, followed by the Feast of Unleavened Bread. Counting from this Feast, after seven weeks, came the Feast of Pentecost (the "fiftieth" day), also called the Feast of First Fruits or the "Feast of Weeks." In the seventh month, the sacred month, three "seasons of holy convocation" occurred; on the first day the Feast of Trumpets, on the tenth the Great Day of Atonement, and on the fifteenth began the Feast of Tabernacles, or Ingathering, continuing for seven days. Moreover, the seventh year was observed as a Sabbatical year, a year of rest for the land. After seven sevens of years, on the year following the seven sevens, the system came to its climax in the great Year of Jubilee.

THE SEVENTH DAY. [Ch. 23:1-3]

All the sacred seasons recorded in this chapter are designated "holy convocations." The term does not apply to the gathering of all the people at a central place of worship, which was required only on the three great Feasts of Passover, Pentecost, and Tabernacles; but it anticipated such local assemblies as in later days met in the synagogues. It certainly meant to prescribe meetings for public worship.

The first of these "holy convocations" was the weekly Sabbath. As it was continually recurring and was the most important of all the sacred seasons, it naturally introduces the whole series, and, indeed, it sums up in itself the meaning and significance of all these "set times of Jehovah."

Its peculiar holiness is emphasized by the prohibition of all labor. The term applied to it is "the Sabbath of rest" or a "Sabbath of solemn rest." On other sacred seasons servile work was forbidden, that is, the cultivation of fields, and the usual daily tasks; but on the Sabbath, and on the Day of Atonement, no work of any kind was allowed.

Two reasons were assigned, one that God had rested on the "seventh day," when the work of creation was complete; the other, that God had delivered Israel from the bondage in Egypt (Deuteronomy 5:15). These two conceptions of rest and redemption appear in the ritual of all these "sacred feasts." The Sabbath day was to be celebrated, not only by release from labor, and by assemblies for worship, but by family gatherings and by relief of the poor. While, as on the Day of Atonement, no work was permitted, it was not to be a day of solemn fasting, but a day of gladness and joy. Like the other "feasts," it was to be a "sign" that Israel belonged to the Lord and had been redeemed and consecrated as his people.

Disobedience to the Sabbath law was certain to result in national disaster; its observance was to mark the "rest" in Canaan which God had promised. In our own land and day Sabbath desecration is endangering the very life of our nation. Sabbath observance is a bulwark of all our most prized and sacred institutions.

The Christian Church keeps as a Sabbath, not the seventh, but the first day of the week. It does so to commemorate the resurrection of Christ, who on that day rose from the dead. It is felt that Christians stand on resurrection ground. They wish to celebrate, not creation, but redemption. The belief is that we are no more bound to a Hebrew Sabbath than to a Hebrew Passover or a Feast of Tabernacles, or the Hebrew sacrifices and ceremonials. We belong to a "New Creation."

On the other hand, not all Christians are bound to the feasts and fasts which have been instituted by various branches of the Christian Church. "Holy days" may be of help to some worshipers; but there is only one divinely appointed Sabbath, one day sacred to rest and worship and to the relief of those in need; one day which calls to mind the work of our Redeemer. There is even a danger that the supreme purpose of this day may be forgotten. The custom of observing one "Sunday" for this purpose, and a second "Sunday" for another purpose, is being commercialized. Whatever "church year" or "Christian year" one may adopt, he should seek so to observe the first day of each week that he will be forcefully reminded of the

Risen Christ, and will recognize anew that by His redeeming work Christ has consecrated us to serve Him who is our Saviour and our Lord. For a Christian the Sabbath day should be supremely "the Lord's Day."

THE FEAST OF PASSOVER AND UNLEAVENED BREAD.
[Ch. 23:4-14]

Strictly speaking, the Sabbath was not a "feast," although it embodied the essence of all the sacred seasons. The first "feast' of the holy year was Passover, with its closely related feast of Unleavened Bread. As the name indicated, the celebration was in memory of the events connected with the deliverance of Israel from bondage in Egypt. On that fateful night the stubborn hearts of the Egyptians were broken by the death of the first-born in every home; but the Angel of Death *passed over* the homes of the Israelites. A lamb had been slain, a life had been substituted for the first-born, the blood had been sprinkled on the lintels and the door-posts of the houses, the families were seated to feast on the lamb; and that night they escaped in haste, not waiting until the bread had been leavened. This protection from judgment and deliverance from bondage were in fulfilment of the divine promise: "When I see the blood, I *will pass over* you, and there shall no plague be upon you to destroy you, when I smite the land of Egypt."

Therefore, for the Hebrew people Passover was the annual Independence Day. It was celebrated by a sacred feast. The central feature was a lamb which had been slain. It was eaten with "bitter herbs" to symbolize the cruel tyranny which had been endured in Egypt, and with unleavened bread to recall the haste of their departure from the land.

The relation of this Passover Feast to the Supper of our Lord is most clear and impressive. Both are memorials of a redemption that is past; both are prophetic of a greater redemption to come. Passover pointed back to a lamb that was slain as a type and symbol, and forward to the coming of the Lamb of God who was to take away the sin of the world. The sacrament looks back to a redemption accomplished by Christ when He came to suffer and to die, but it also predicts His reappearance in glory, for as often as we eat the bread and drink the wine, which commemorate the redemption of "Christ our Passover," we do "shew the Lord's death, till he come."

The Feast of Unleavened Bread was a continuation of the Passover. It began on the following day and lasted a full week. The period was one of rejoicing and fellowship. The first and last days were observed by "holy convocations." On these days no "servile work" could be performed. On each day a "burnt offering," a "meal offering" and a "drink offering" were presented unto the Lord for "a sweet savour." They were symbols of consecration and communion.

The two characteristic features of the feast, however, were (1) the exclusion of leaven and (2) the ritual of the peace-offering.

(1) Leaven was a symbol of moral corruption. During the entire continuance of the feast it must not, on pain of death, appear in any Hebrew home. So scrupulous were the people in this regard that before the feast began they swept every part of their houses to discover and remove every fragment of leaven. The meaning of the prohibition was quite evident. Israel had observed

the Passover to recall their redemption; now as a redeemed people they must be a holy people. They could
not accept that which was corrupt. They must exclude
all evil from among them.

Most forcefully does Paul apply to the lives of Christians the principle involved in these symbols: "Purge out
therefore the old leaven, that ye may be a new lump, as
ye are unleavened. For even Christ our passover is sacrificed for us: therefore let us keep the feast, not with old
leaven, neither with the leaven of malice and wickedness;
but with the unleavened bread of sincerity and truth"
(I Corinthians 5:7, 8).

(2) The other feature of the ritual of the Feast of
Unleavened Bread was the presenting of a "sheaf of
first-fruits." This was to be done, during the feast, "on
the morrow after the sabbath." Many suppose that this
offering of the sheaf of the first ripe barley constituted a
separate festival which they designate as the "feast of
first-fruits." That title, however, belongs to the feast
which follows, namely, Pentecost; but the waving of the
"sheaf of first-fruits" was an essential feature of the feast
of Unleavened Bread.

It is true that this formed no part of the original
institution of "Passover" and its related feast (Exodus
12:1-20). Nor could it be observed in the wilderness,
where no grain was being sown or reaped. It was a prospective feature of the feast, and was introduced by a
distinct formula: "When ye have come into the land."
This is the third of four instances in Leviticus in which a
law is recorded which could not be observed until the
people had entered the land of Canaan (14:34; 19:23;
23:10; 25:2).

It was, however, a very important and significant

feature of the feast. The ordinance was this: "Ye shall bring a sheaf of the first-fruits of your harvest unto the priest, and he shall wave the sheaf before the Lord to be accepted for you." Another rendering is: "Ye shall bring the first-fruit *omer* of your harvest." This would mean that the priest would not be required to wave a literal sheaf of barley, but some six pints of barley flour. With this flour, according to the ancient practise, there was mixed a quantity of oil and a handful of frankincense. This was presented as a meal offering. It was all "waved" before the Lord, that is, by a familiar gesture all was held out to the Lord horizontally toward the altar, and then brought back. A portion was burned on the altar; the rest was eaten by the worshipers. The meaning was clear. The very first of the ripe harvest was waved before the Lord, to indicate that the entire harvest belonged to Him. It was received again from the Lord as a symbol that He was the giver of the harvest. It was shared with the Lord and the worshipers to indicate fellowship with Him and His people, and enjoyment of all His gracious gifts.

For the Christian the principle involved is plain and important. The first and best of all our possessions should be offered to the Lord; but when we present our tithes or portions of our income, it does not mean that fraction alone belongs to God and the rest to us. Rather it is a symbol that all belongs to Him, and must be used in fellowship with Him and in the service of others. The first-fruits were a promise and an earnest of the coming harvest. The ritual gave assurance that all the harvest would be reaped, all would come from God, all must be used so as to meet with His approval and in fellowship with Him.

The use of the term "first-fruits" by the Apostle Paul

had given to this feature of the feast a deep significance. When presenting the great truth of resurrection, he declared that as Christ rose from the dead "on the morrow after the Sabbath," He became "the first-fruits of them that are asleep." His resurrection assures the resurrection of all who belong to Him. "Because he lives we shall live also."

Thus Passover and the Feast of Unleavened Bread may picture to the believer both the death of Christ our Paschal Lamb, and also the resurrection of Christ, the First-fruits of them that are asleep, Christ our Sacrifice and Christ our Life.

THE FEAST OF PENTECOST. [Ch. 23:15-22]

After the sheaf of first-fruits had been "waved before the Lord," seven weeks were counted. Then, on the fiftieth day, came the Feast of Pentecost (Greek "fiftieth"). This was a harvest festival. As the sheaf of first-fruits represented the beginning of the barley harvest, so Pentecost marked the completion of the wheat harvest. Yet it was much more than a harvest festival. Unlike the harvest feasts of pagan nations which celebrated the forces of nature, this was a sacred season observed in worship of him who is "Ruler of all nature." It was a day of "holy convocation." All "servile work" was prohibited. Two "wave loaves," baked with leaven, were offered to the Lord. These were accompanied by a sin offering, a burnt offering, and peace offerings, representing expiation, dedication, and communion.

The main feature of the ritual for the day consisted in the presentation of the two "wave loaves." These represented the first-fruits of the completed grain harvest.

By offering them the people acknowledged the divine Lord who had given the harvest, to whom all the harvest belonged, and by whom their daily bread was supplied. The presenting of these loaves gave to the feast one of its appropriate names, the "Feast of First-fruits," just as the "Feast of Weeks" and the "Feast of Pentecost" were names which gave the exact time of the observance.

In harmony with the thanksgiving and rejoicing of this feast, and as symbolized by its peace offerings and wave offerings, the ritual recognized the need of making provision for the poor. This was a harvest festival, but no one must believe that the produce of his field belonged to himself alone. All came from God and was to be shared with those in need: "And when ye reap the harvest of your land, thou shalt not make clean riddance of the corners of thy field when thou reapest, neither shalt thou gather any gleaning of thy harvest: thou shalt leave them unto the poor, and to the stranger: I am the Lord your God" (v. 22; so 19:9, 10).

Like the feasts of Passover and Unleavened Bread, the Feast of Pentecost rightly is regarded as typical. Passover symbolized the death of Christ and the "sheaf of first-fruits" His resurrection; so the "wave-loaves" may represent His Church, formed by His Spirit, on the Day of Pentecost, fifty days after His resurrection from the dead.

The loaves were two in number, possibly typifying the two component parts of the church, Jews and Gentiles, united in Christ. The loaves were leavened, and it is true that a measure of evil adheres in all the members of the Christian Church. Yet the loaves were accompanied by a sin offering, in view of which they were acceptable to God. So Christians are in need of atonement and are "accepted in the beloved."

That these loaves, presented to the Lord at this Feast of First-fruits, represent the church might appear also from the use of the term in the New Testament, in which Christians are called the "first-fruits of God's creatures" (James 1:18) and in which Paul declares, in reference to the Jewish members of the church, "And if the first-fruit is holy, so is the lump."

On that Day of Pentecost which followed the resurrection of Christ, the Holy Spirit used the preaching of Peter in the conversion of three thousand souls, and by the same Spirit these believers were all bound together into one body, the Church of Christ. It is natural that the followers of Christ regard Pentecost as the birthday of the church.

Among the early Christians the anniversary of the day was regarded as a fitting time to receive candidates into the membership of the church. These candidates were clothed in white, and the day came to be called White Sunday or "Whit Sunday."

In a real sense the Christian Pentecost has not ended. Where the same Gospel preached by Peter is proclaimed, the same Spirit is present to touch the hearts of hearers and to baptize them into the one body of believers, the Church of the living God. This Christian Pentecost is prophetic: as this was the feast of "first-fruits," so believers are the pledge and earnest of the great ingathering, the completed harvest, when "the fulness of the Gentiles is come in."

THE FEAST OF TRUMPETS. [Ch. 23:23-25]

As the seventh day is holy, and as the seventh week was followed by the Feast of Pentecost, so the seventh month was the sacred month. Its arrival was announced by the Feast of Trumpets on the first day; the tenth day was the Great Day of Atonement, and on the fifteenth day was begun the Feast of Tabernacles.

The people of God must not confuse sanctity with sadness. The "sacred month" did have features which, as on the Day of Atonement, were solemn and searching, but the seventh month was celebrated with rejoicing and thanksgiving.

This surely was true of the Feast of Trumpets. It was the glad New Year Festival, for it ushered in the first month of the civil year. It was a "sabbath," on which no unnecessary work was to be done; it was to be observed by a "holy convocation"; sacrifices were to be offered to the Lord; yet, most of all, it was to be a day of festivity and gladness. The sounding of trumpets set the key-note of joy.

The most charming picture of this "first day of the seventh month" is given by the historian Nehemiah.

On this day, when the restored exiles heard the law of God read by Ezra the scribe, they realized their unworthiness, and "the people wept when they heard the words of the law"; but Ezra and Nehemiah and the priests cheered them with the words: "This day is holy unto the Lord your God; mourn not nor weep, . . . neither be ye sorry; for the joy of the Lord is your strength. . . . And all the people went their way to eat and to drink, and to send portions, and to make great mirth, because

they understood the words that were declared unto them"
(Nehemiah 8:9-12).

This Feast of Trumpets, accordingly, is taken by
some readers as a graphic symbol of the preaching of the
Gospel. Its arresting call did announce the Day of Atonement, with its summons to repentance and with its solemn ritual; but the ancient festival had as its chief
message the arrival of the most joyous of all seasons. It
found its essential expression in the seven appointed days
of unclouded rejoicing during the Feast of Tabernacles,
the happiest and most cherished days of all the sacred
year. Repentance and faith in Christ, when one responds
to the Gospel call, is followed not by a fast, but by a feast.
To him comes the word of the ancient historian: "The
joy of the Lord is your strength."

Other symbolic suggestions, related to the trumpet,
are found in New Testament imagery. It is at the sound
of a trumpet that the dead in Christ are to rise; at the
sound of a trumpet signaling His return His people are
to be gathered from the four quarters of the earth. At
the sounding of the seventh angel the triumphant voice
is heard: "The kingdoms of this world are become the
kingdom of our Lord, and of his Christ; and he shall
reign for ever and for ever."

THE DAY OF ATONEMENT. [Ch. 23:26-32]

The ritual of this solemn celebration already has been
set forth in impressive detail (Ch. 16). Reference here is
made to the appointed day to intimate the relation of this
ritual to the other sacred seasons. It is this relation which
brings its serious message to all who have learned of the
atonement made for us by Christ, our Great High Priest.

The day was one of complete rest: "Ye shall do no manner of work" (v. 13). It was to be observed also by "an holy convocation." Yet its supreme purpose was to indicate the provision God had made for the expiation of the sins of all the people. The ceremonial of that day represented the complete removal of those sins and the restoration of the people to the fellowship and worship of God.

However, there was a definite condition on which one might partake of the atonement that had been provided. That condition was sincere repentance and sorrow for sin and trust in the pardon and grace of God. It is this condition which is repeated and emphasized in this paragraph of the law. "Ye shall afflict your souls, and offer an offering made by fire unto the Lord" (v. 27).

The Feast of Trumpets had announced the opening of the New Year, the first day of the most joyful of all months, and the near approach of the glad Feast of Tabernacles. No one, however, could share this joy and gladness who had not repented of his sins and accepted God's provision for atonement. Therefore here is emphasized the absolute need of expressing penitence and faith by "afflicting their souls," that is by a solemn fast. This is enforced by an arresting threat: "For whatsoever soul it be that shall not be afflicted in that same day, he shall be cut off from among his people" (v. 29).

Such, indeed, is the truth. One who is to enjoy the boundless blessings of the Christian life, and is to realize the benefit of Christ's atoning work, can do so only as he fulfils the requirement of sincere sorrow for sin and submissive obedience to Christ.

One who at the Feast of Trumpets has heard the Gospel call, and wishes to partake of the fruit and festivities of the Feast of Tabernacles must experience the penitence required on the Day of Atonement.

Such, for example, was the message of Peter as he proclaimed the Gospel on the Day of Pentecost: "Repent and be baptized every one of you in the name of Jesus Christ for the remission of sins, and ye shall receive the gift of the Holy Ghost" (Acts 2:38).

THE FEAST OF TABERNACLES. [Ch. 23:33-44]

Tabernacles are tents, or booths, or huts made from the branches of trees. When the Israelites had settled in the land of promise, they celebrated every year a feast, during which time they left their houses and lived in such tabernacles, or temporary shelters.

This Feast of Booths or Tabernacles was the most joyful of all the sacred seasons and formed the climax of the annual religious festivals. It was observed from the fifteenth to the twenty-second day of the seventh month (October). Two reasons were assigned for this celebration. One was that it marked the end of the agricultural year. All the produce had been gathered in, not only the harvests of grain, but the products of the vine and of the fruit trees. The feast, therefore, also was called the Feast of Ingathering. It was for the Hebrews the national "Harvest Home." It finds its counterpart in our modern Thanksgiving Day. Thus it was a season of rejoicing, of family reunions and of gratitude to God. It began with "an holy convocation," and closed with a similar religious service on the eighth day. Amid all the rejoicing the sacred character of the feast was maintained. Thanksgiving to God as the Giver of all good was expressed by an unusual number of sacrifices. During the course of the week, some seventy bullocks were presented as offerings, together with the sacrifices of lambs and rams and the presenting of meal-offerings and drink-offerings in proportion.

Gratitude to God for the harvest was the second reason for the celebration. It was to recall the goodness of God to His people during their wanderings in the wilderness. To bring to mind those days, the Israelites dwelt in booths or tabernacles during the week of the feast, as they had dwelt during all those long years of their wilderness wanderings. Then they had no fields or harvests, no vineyards or olive trees. Yet God sustained them. He fed them with "manna" or "bread from heaven," and taught them that "man doth not live by bread only, but by every word that proceedeth out of the mouth of God" (Deuteronomy 8:3). This was the annually recurring message of this harvest festival.

When the seven days of the feast had ended, they were followed by a second "holy convocation." It marked a day of holy rest, and was not only the close of the Feast of Tabernacles but the conclusion of the whole series of annual festivals and feasts.

Like Passover and Pentecost, this Feast of Trumpets is also regarded as symbolic and prophetic. Pentecost as a feast of first-fruits was an earnest of the completed harvest. So the "first-fruits" which form the Christian Church are the earnest of the great feast of "Ingathering," when at last all nations shall be brought into the garner of God.

The Gospel proclamation of the Feast of Trumpets will result in the repentance of Israel on a Great Day of Atonement, and all the peoples of the earth will rejoice

in a Feast of Tabernacles, the age of blessedness and
peace (Romans 11:25).

THE HOLY LIGHT, THE HOLY BREAD, THE HOLY NAME. [Ch. 24]

The question is raised as to why this chapter, with
its diverse subjects, follows the regulations as to the *Times
for Worship* and precedes the instructions as to the *Sabbatical Year* and the *Year of Jubilee*, which also are sacred
seasons. It is not unnatural, however, that ordinances for
worship in the various seasons of the year should be followed by instructions as to certain features of daily worship. Then again the laws relative to using the products
of the fields and vineyards and orchards are here suc-
ceeded by statutes for the sacred use of certain portions
of grain and of olives. Nor is it surprising that regulations
relative to sacred seasons should be interrupted by a
chapter which deals with the Holy Light and Holy Bread
of the sanctuary, and with the Holy Name of God.

The *Holy Light* (vs. 1-4) was to be provided by olive
oil which was to burn continually in the lamps of the
golden "candlestick" or *lampstand*. This beautiful piece
of sacred furniture was placed on the south side of the
Holy Place, a curtained room which had no other source
of light. The "candlestick" was made of pure gold. A
central shaft supported six branches. This shaft, like the
lateral branches, ended in a cup shaped like an almond
blossom and prepared to hold the oil, which must be
burned continually from evening until morning, under
the special care of the High Priest. The oil was made
from olives provided by the people. It was to be "pure,"
and was "beaten." That is, it was produced by crushing

the olives in a process which secured oil of the highest quality, for worshipers must always present to the Lord the very best they can provide.

The meaning of symbols is made plain in both the Old Testament and the New. The people of God were to be the source of spiritual light in a dark world. For this high service they needed to be filled with the Spirit of God, of which oil was the scriptural symbol.

Thus the prophet Zechariah recorded his vision of the golden "candlestick" supplied with oil from two olive trees. It represented Israel, appointed to give light to the nations, but wholly dependent on the grace supplied by the Spirit of God; for the message was this: "Not by might, nor by power, but by my Spirit, saith the Lord" (Zech. 4:1-14).

A similar vision was reported by the Apostle John. He saw seven golden "candlesticks," representing the collective church of all the centuries. "In the midst of the seven candlesticks one like unto the Son of man" stood, clothed in priestly garments, ready like Aaron of old, to keep and trim the lamps, and to supply them with oil, that they might fulfil their high function expressed in his own memorable words: "Ye are the light of the world." For all of His people it is possible to enjoy this exalted privilege and to "shine as lights in the world," as they "worship by the Spirit of God, and rejoice in Christ Jesus" (Revelation 1:12-20; Philippians 3:3. R.V.).

Then there was the *Holy Bread* (vs. 5-9). Twelve loaves, representing the twelve tribes of Israel, were placed on the golden table, in the Holy Place, opposite the golden candlestick. These loaves were arranged in two rows or "piles," and between them was a bowl of frankincense. Every Sabbath day fresh loaves were provided and those which were removed were eaten in the Holy Place by the priests. The incense was burned as "an offering made by fire unto the Lord."

These loaves, or "cakes," made of fine flour, were known as "shew bread"; more exactly, the term means *"bread of the presence,"* that is, of God. Just beyond the veil was the "mercy-seat," and the "glory" symbolic of the divine majesty. The incense was a symbol of worship, and the loaves represented the daily labor and service of the people of God who were ever in His presence, and who presented these loaves as a thank offering in recognition of His protection and care.

The fact that the priests were permitted to eat the loaves in the sanctuary was to signify that, while all our tasks are performed in the presence of the Lord, and while we present to Him the fruits of our labor, He graciously supplies us with needed nourishment and food. We consecrate to Him the fruit of our toil and we trust Him to give us each day "our daily bread."

There are those who love to find in the sacred loaves a type of the perfect obedience of Christ, who was wholly dedicated to the service of God and who is, indeed, the Bread of His Presence, the Bread of the world, the Bread of Life.

These ordinances relating to the Holy Light and the Holy Bread are followed by a tragic incident related to the *Holy Name* (vs. 10-23). "The son of an Israelitish woman, whose father was an Egyptian, went out among the children of Israel," or as some translate, "went out into the midst of the children of Israel," that is, he lived outside the camp and came where he had no right to be. "And the son of the Israelitish woman blasphemed the *name* and cursed: and they brought him to Moses."

Two questions needed to be settled: (1) What should be the penalty for blasphemy? (2) Should the same penalty apply to Israelites and non-Israelites alike.

Moses declared that the penalty should be death, and that the law, like the laws which follow (vs. 17-21), were binding equally on the home-born and the "stranger."

These laws relating to murder, to killing a neighbor's beast, and for injuring a neighbor, had been announced earlier (Exodus 21:12, 23-26), but are repeated here to show that, as just indicated, they should apply to all, whether or not they were Israelites by birth.

The severity of these laws has been criticized and particularly because they involve the principle of the *lex talionis*, that is, "life for life, breach for breach, eye for eye, tooth for tooth." This law is said to have been abrogated by our Lord in His Sermon on the Mount (Matthew 5:38-42).

It should be remembered that our Saviour was not considering a principle of civil law, but was condemning a spirit of retaliation and revenge. The law of Moses did not authorize private and irresponsible retaliation, nor did our Saviour forbid all resort to legal processes; nor did He question the general principle that "the penalty should fit the crime."

The Jews never interpreted the words literally, except in the case of blasphemy. In this incident the death sentence was pronounced and executed. The witnesses laid their hands on the head of the offender to indicate that they had no complicity in the crime and that upon him devolved the responsibility for his own death.

Whatever may be said in criticism of so severe a sentence, there should be in this incident a solemn warning against blasphemy. The name of God is not a mere title or phrase. It denotes all that by which God has re-vealed himself to man. It includes all that God has shown Himself to be. Nothing is more perilous or more injurious to a community or a nation than irreverence towards things which are sacred. Profanity and blasphemy are sins which involve exceptional guilt. Reverence to-ward God is the foundation not only of religion but of morality. There is a message for the present day even in this tragic episode which emphasizes the need for rev-erencing the *Holy Name*.

The Sabbatical Year. [Ch. 25:1-7]

The series of sacred seasons appointed for the Israel-ites included not only a seventh day, and a seventh week, and a seventh month, but a seventh year, the "Sabbatical Year," and following seven sevens of years came the "Year of Jubilee." The calendar of annual festivals (Ch. 23) was separated from the ordinance for the Sab-batical Year and for Jubilee (Ch. 25) by mention of the light and the bread for the sanctuary and the punishment for blasphemy (Ch. 24). Yet this separation is instruc-tive, and the order is not altogether without harmony. Unlike the annual festivals, the Sabbatical Year and Jubilee were not marked by "holy convocations," they al-lowed all kinds of labor except that which was strictly agricultural, and while related to harvests, they were not concerned with fruit or grain or products, but specifically with the *land*. It therefore is not surprising that regula-tions relating to the holy light and the holy bread and the holy name, should be followed by laws concerning the holy land. These laws emphasized the fact that not only the time, and the labor and the food of Israel belonged to the Lord, but also the land.

This was true particularly of the Sabbatical Year. Its ordinance was as follows: "And the Lord spake unto Moses in mount Sinai, saying, Speak unto the children of Israel, and say unto them, When ye come into the land which I give you, then shall the land keep a sabbath unto the Lord. Six years thou shalt sow thy field, and six years thou shalt prune thy vineyard, and gather in the fruit thereof; but in the seventh year shall be a sabbath of rest unto the land, a sabbath for the Lord: thou shalt neither sow thy field, nor prune thy vineyard. That which groweth of its own accord of thy harvest thou shalt not reap, neither gather the grapes of thy vine undressed: for it is a year of rest unto the land" (Ch. 25:1-5).

Thus this law was prospective. It could not be brought into operation until the people had "come into the land" of promise. The year was to be dedicated to the Lord. It was to be a sacred season. As the weekly Sabbath recognized God as the Creator of the world, so this Sabbatical Year recognized God as the Owner of the land. The spontaneous products, "that which groweth of itself," were not to be harvested nor to be hoarded; but it was further provided that such produce was to be left in the fields for the free use of all persons and also for the cattle (vs. 6, 7). The mention of "cattle" indicates clearly that this was not a communistic law, but required that for a time all exclusive rights of individual owners were suspended; rich and poor were placed on an equality and the great truth was emphasized that the land belonged to the Lord and to Him account must be made for its use.

THE YEAR OF JUBILEE. [Ch. 25:8-55]

The truth that the land was the property of their God, and that the people were merely his tenants, was further emphasized by the ordinance of the Year of Jubilee. This formed the supreme and unique climax and culmination of all the series of sacred seasons. In the statutes of no other nation was there a provision for a time of such universal relief and gladness and joy. The ordinance embodies principles which might go far toward solving the social problems of the present day. In general, the provisions were as follows: "And thou shalt number seven sabbaths of years unto thee, seven times seven years; and the space of the seven sabbaths of years shall be unto thee forty and nine years.

"Then shalt thou cause the trumpet of the jubilee to sound on the tenth day of the seventh month, in the day of atonement shall ye make the trumpet sound throughout all your land.

"And ye shall hallow the fiftieth year, and proclaim liberty throughout all the land unto all the inhabitants thereof: it shall be a jubilee unto you; and ye shall return every man unto his possession, and ye shall return every man unto his family.

"A jubilee shall that fiftieth year be unto you: ye shall not sow, neither reap that which groweth of itself in it, nor gather the grapes in it of thy vine undressed.

"For it is the jubilee; it shall be holy unto you: ye shall eat the increase thereof out of the field" (Ch. 25:8-12).

The most familiar, and most significant sentence of

the ordinance is this: "*Proclaim liberty throughout the land unto all the inhabitants thereof.*"

This "liberty" meant not only freedom for slaves, but freedom from depressing toil, and liberty to return to the land of which any one had been dispossessed.

First of all, the law is applied to the *ownership of the land* (vs. 13-28). The conquered country of Canaan was to be divided by lot among the Israelites, and the portion which came to each family could never be permanently alienated. As specifically stated, "The land shall not be sold *forever* (that is, "in perpetuity"); for the land is mine; for ye are strangers and sojourners with me." This divine prescription meant that God claimed to be the supreme owner of the land, and as such He could impose the conditions on which the land could be held by His tenants. Among other conditions was this, namely, that in the year of Jubilee all property in land returned to its original proprietors. This condition determined the value of landed property. The price would be greater or less, proportioned to the time which would elapse between the time of purchase and the next "Year of Jubilee."

Furthermore, provision was made for the *redemption* of land. This might be done by the former tenant in case he became able so to do, or by someone near of kin, who might secure the land for himself and thus retain it as a possession of the family. In fact, it was regarded as the duty of the nearest relative to redeem the property which the poverty of the kinsman had compelled him to sell. It became a custom, almost obligatory, for such a "kinsman-redeemer" to marry the childless widow of a former owner.

These provisions interpret the lovely idyl of Ruth and Boaz. A "redeemer" must be "near of kin"; he must be rich enough to pay the price; he must be willing to redeem. All these conditions were fulfilled by Boaz, who married Ruth and became the ancestor of our Lord Jesus Christ. All these qualifications too were met by our Lord Himself. He became a man, our "Elder Brother"; His precious blood was "rich enough to pay the price of sin"; He was willing to lay down His life for us. He had "power to lay it down, and power to take it again." Each one of us should claim Him as our Redeemer.

The law of Jubilee was next applied to the ownership of *dwelling houses* (vs. 29-34). Those in walled cities were not the creation or the special allotment of God, as was true of the land. Therefore, they could be redeemed within a year after the date of sale, but would not revert to the previous owner in the year of Jubilee.

Houses in villages were regarded as part of the landed property, and, like the land on which they were built, they were subject to the law of Jubilee. This likewise was true of the houses of Levites, who lived in cities but possessed no land. In order that they might have permanent homes they could apply to their houses the same provisions of Jubilee as were applied to land by the members of other tribes.

A third application of the law of Jubilee was to *slavery* (vs. 39-55). The subject was introduced by a paragraph which warns against all severity and heartlessness in matters of finance. If a brother has become poor and burdened with debt no interest is to be exacted from him. He is to be treated with kindness and to be given help lest he be driven to sell himself into practical or actual slavery. The Israelites were reminded that recently they all had been slaves in Egypt, and were delivered by the mercy of God. As servants of God they should be merciful to their fellow servants (vs. 35-37).

Moses did not abolish slavery. He did establish laws which vastly improved the condition of slaves and he taught principles in accordance with which slavery, in time, was forbidden. According to the Mosaic code, man-stealing was treated as a crime punishable by death. A slave was no mere chattel. Not his person but his labor belonged to his master. "Thou shalt not make him to serve as a bondservant; as an hired servant, and as a sojourner, he shall be with thee" (v. 39). Most important of all, the law of Jubilee required that in that year all slaves should "go out free."

These laws applied to such as were in bondage to fellow Israelites. In case, however, a Hebrew was in slavery to a foreign resident of the land he always could claim the sacred right of redemption. Either by money of his own, or by such as was furnished by a near relative, he could purchase his freedom. The amount to be paid was in proportion to the number of years remaining before the next year of Jubilee; for in that year he, in any case, must be set free.

It is true that the law of Jubilee did not apply to slaves from other nations. Yet these must be treated humanely and were protected from violence and tyranny (Exodus 21:20, 21, 26, 27).

However regulated, slavery was recognized by Moses as an established institution. It exists in the world today. Only by the influence of Christ will men recognize fully the rights of their fellow men. There is one rule which will end tyranny and oppression: "Bear ye one another's burdens and so fulfil the law of Christ."

It also may be admitted that the law of Jubilee, with

such provisions as the reversion of landed property, did not insure social justice or absolute equality of privilege and opportunity. It did limit the acquisition of vast amounts of wealth and also the suffering of extreme poverty. None could become very rich, none need to be pitifully poor. However, this law did protect the rights of private property. It did not encourage shiftless dependence and idleness, nor did it deny to thrift and industry the just rewards of comfort and increasing wealth.

The Year of Jubilee began with the Day of Atonement. It brought to the people of God freedom, restoration, reunion, rest and joy. The true Year of Jubilee is yet to come. The completed atonement is to be followed by the perfect age of deliverance, of freedom "from the bondage of corruption," of the "liberty of the sons of God." The world awaits its age of rest and rejoicing. Its hope lies in the coming of the Kinsman-Redeemer, "whom the heaven must receive until the *times of the restitution of all things,* which God hath spoken by the mouth of all his holy prophets since the world began" (Acts 3:21).

IV

CONCLUSION

Promises and Warnings. [Ch. 26]

The first two verses of this chapter have been regarded as properly belonging to the previous paragraph. They set forth two fundamental principles of the Hebrew law, namely to abstain from idol worship and to observe the Sabbath. It has been supposed that the verses refer to the temptations to break the law which would confront Israelites who had sold themselves to heathen masters and would be confronted continually with idolatrous practises.

On the other hand, this brief summary of the First Table of the Law (the first Four Commandments) forms a proper basis for the promises and warnings which now follow. These are based on obedience to the law which was the condition of the covenant God had made with Israel. Accordingly there follow, first, promises of blessing in case of obedience (vs. 3-13); second, threats of punishment for the disobedient (vs. 14-39), and, third, the assurance that God would "remember" His "covenant" in dealing with a repentant remnant of His people (vs. 40-45).

1. The *promises* were of the most glowing character. Rain would be given and fruitful seasons, and harvests so rich that "the threshing shall reach unto the vintage, and the vintage shall reach unto the sowing time." Peace

would be assured. There would be no fear of wild beasts within the land, or of enemies from without. Should the nation be attacked, "five of you shall chase one hundred, and an hundred of you shall put ten thousand to flight." According to the covenant, their numbers would be increased, and the harvests become so proportionately great that the remaining produce of one year would need to be removed from the storehouses to make room for the new. Best of all, the presence of God would be with them: "I will walk among you, and will be your God, and ye shall be my people."

2. These promises of blessing were followed by *warnings* and by threats of appalling calamities which would be visited on disobedience to the divine commandments. The people would be smitten by disease, the harvests would be consumed by their enemies. Instead of putting to flight a thousand, it was said, "Ye shall flee when none pursueth you." Instead of abundant rains, the heaven would be as iron and the earth as brass. The people would suffer from plagues and wild beasts and famine.

Four series of threats are recorded, each beginning with the phrase, "If ye shall not hearken," and each repeating the formula, "I will chastise you seven times for your sins." The phrase "seven times" is not to be taken in a numerical sense. Rather, the sacred number symbolizes an increasing severity, and the awful thoroughness and completeness of the divine judgments.

Not only would there be famine, but famine of such a character that the people would eat the flesh of their own sons and daughters. The high places of idol worship would be destroyed, and the dead bodies of worshipers be heaped on the fallen idols. The cities and the sanctuaries would be in ruins, and the whole land be so desolate that even the Hebrews' enemies would be amazed. The people would not be permitted to linger in the desolated country but would be scattered among the nations. This would be by the very action of God Himself, who would drive them out with a drawn sword. The land would enjoy the sabbaths of rest which Israel in disobedience had not allowed.

In the lands of their enemies they would find no relief. They would live in continual fear and terror and matchless misery. They would be so submerged by the surrounding peoples that their identity largely would be lost: "Ye shall perish among the heathen, and the land of your enemies shall eat you up" (v. 38).

3. However, they should not be absolutely destroyed; a remnant would be saved: "When they be in the land of their enemies, I will not cast them away, neither will I abhor them to destroy them utterly." If and when they repent, if their hard hearts are humbled, if they admit the justice of their punishment, God will be mindful of His covenant. The words are these: "Then will I remember my covenant with Jacob, and also my covenant with Isaac, and also my covenant with Abraham will I remember; and I will remember the land" (v. 42).

This conditional promise has been interpreted as a positive prediction. It is understood by some persons that the land of Palestine belongs to the Jews irrespective of their obedience to the commandments of God or their acceptance of His Son. Consequently, many theories are held concerning the "Return of the Jews" or the "Restoration of Israel." These theories are so diverse and conflicting as to intimate the need of great caution, of deep humility, and of abounding charity in attempting to solve the problems of prophecy.

As the Old Testament promises relate not only to the "Jews," that is, to the descendants of Judah and Benjamin, but also to all Israel, it is contended that the land in question belongs to the Twelve Tribes, and therefore the Ten Tribes are not "lost" but only "concealed," and that they will be found and united with the "Jews." Thus there are large groups of Jews and Christians who believe that the Anglo-Saxon peoples are the Ten Tribes, specifically, that Great Britain is Ephraim and the United States Manasseh, and that these nations are to dominate the earth.

Others hold that Zionism and the present rehabilitation of Palestine and the assurance of a home land for the Jews are in fulfilment of the promises to Israel.

Still others believe that after the future "Coming of Christ" and the resurrection of the dead, the Jews will be given the land of Palestine, and there will re-establish the ritual and renew the animal sacrifices with which the Book of Leviticus so largely deals.

More commonly it is understood that the Hebrew sacrifices were symbolic and typical and were fulfilled "once for all" in the perfect atonement of Christ. It is believed that the hope for Jews and Gentiles alike lies in repentance and in obedience to the divine Messiah. In Him all believers form one "body," where distinctions of race no longer exist. The true Israelites are those who are "Christ's"; they are "Abraham's seed and heirs according to the promise." They claim the boundless blessings which belong to the New Covenant. They are not "mindful of" any "country from which they came out; . . . they desire a better country, that is an heavenly;

wherefore God is not ashamed to be called their God."
"They shall inherit the earth," yet their highest expecta-
tion is to "behold the land that is very far off" and to
"see the King in his beauty."

V

APPENDIX

CONCERNING VOLUNTARY VOWS. [Ch. 27]

To A book like Leviticus, concerned with definite requirements as to worship and the lives of worshipers, it is natural, even necessary, that there should be appended regulations in respect to vows. These, by way of contrast to such ordinances, were not required by law, but were purely voluntary; however, when made, they were regarded as solemn pledges to God. The Mosaic legislation neither required nor forbade such vows.

According to the New Testament, there is no place in Christian practise for exactly such pledges. A Christian can do no more than his duty, he should never do less. He can promise no more than complete consecration to Christ. However, a review of these Levitical regulations, given under a system of laws which made such voluntary vows possible, should lead the followers of Christ to regard with deep reverence those promises which popularly, and in a sense correctly, are known as "vows." For example, there are obligations assumed in marriage, in baptism, in church membership, in ordination. Such promises, and many others, are vows which are never to be broken or recalled.

On the other hand, the vows made according to the law of Moses could be redeemed, and this "*Appendix*" to Leviticus specifies what objects could be vowed, and under what conditions there could be a redemption or a "commutation" of vows.

It was allowable to dedicate to the Lord either persons, domestic animals, houses, or land; but not "firstlings" or "devoted things" or "tithes," for the obvious reason that the latter already belonged to the Lord.

As to the vowing of *persons* (vs. 1-8), this consisted in consecrating to the service of God certain persons with the evident purpose of redeeming them with money, according to the value placed on them by law. The regulation was as follows: "When a man shall make a singular vow [or, better translated, "shall consecrate a vow"] the persons shall be for the Lord by thy estimation." This "estimation" was proportionate to the sex and age of the persons. Here was no remote intimation of slavery or sacrifice. What was given to the Lord was the value of the labor or services of the dedicated persons. Men were regarded as capable of more labor than women, and mature persons more than children. In case a man was too poor to pay the estimated price for redemption, he could appear before the priest. After examination, a fine was imposed according to his ability to pay, and the money was devoted to the use of the sanctuary.

When a *domestic animal* was dedicated in a vow, if it was fit for sacrifice, it was used as an offering. No substitution was to be made of a bad for a good beast, or even of a good for a bad, otherwise both would be regarded as belonging to the Lord.

In case an "unclean animal," unfit for sacrifice, was dedicated, it could be sold and the proceeds be appropriated for sacred services. Or, in this case, a man who had made the vow could redeem the animal but pay as a fine one-fifth more than the estimated value (vs. 9-13).

Houses and *fields* could be consecrated by a vow, and also might be redeemed. In the case of a house, it must be examined and the price set by the priest. If the owner himself wished to redeem it, he would be compelled to pay one-fifth more than the value determined (vs. 14, 15).

For the possible redemption of a field dedicated by a vow a distinction was made between property which had been inherited and property which had been secured by purchase.

In the former case, the portion dedicated to the Lord was valued by the priest according to the amount of seed required for sowing the field. In case the vow went into effect immediately after the Year of Jubilee, the full price must be paid in redeeming the property. If it was at a later date, the price would be reduced according to the number of years which had elapsed between the previous Jubilee and the time when the vow was made. The field could be redeemed by paying the estimated value, plus one-fifth of such price.

If the owner refused to redeem the land, or if he secretly sold the property to another purchaser, all claim to redemption would be forfeited forever. At the next Year of Jubilee the field would pass into the permanent possession of the priest.

In the case of land acquired by purchase, if it was dedicated to the service of the Lord, it would be valued according to the number of crops it might produce up to the next Year of Jubilee, for on that year it would revert to the original owner. In order to redeem such land, the full amount must be paid at once, and could not be paid in small yearly instalments, as was possible in the case of a field which had been received as an inheritance. In the Year of Jubilee the land did not revert to the purchaser but to the hereditary owner from whom it had been bought by the one who had made the vow.

The proceeds of these vows was to be used in the service of the sanctuary; accordingly all estimates and payments were to be made according to the standard weight of the "shekel of the sanctuary" (vs. 14-25).

Last of all, instructions are given concerning *exclusions from the vow*. According to a law already recorded, all the "first-born" belonged to the Lord (Exodus 13:11-15). It was evident, therefore, that *"firstlings"* could not be dedicated by a vow to the Lord, for already they were His. However, the "firstling" of an animal which was not qualified for sacrifice could be redeemed at a price determined by the priest with the addition of one-fifth of the valuation. If not redeemed it could be sold to anyone who would buy it at this price, the proceeds to be devoted to the sanctuary (vs. 26, 27).

"Devoted things," such as persons condemned to death, or things placed under "the ban," could not be consecrated by a vow, neither could they be sold or redeemed. To such "devoted" things no one could make a personal claim without incurring the penalty of himself being "devoted" or placed under the ban. Thus, when the persons and property of Jericho had been "devoted" to the Lord, Achan was punished for appropriating a wedge of gold and a valuable garment. All such devoted property was not destroyed but used in the service of the sanctuary and for the support of the priesthood (vs. 28, 29).

Most obviously of all, *tithes* could not be dedicated to the Lord by vows, for they were His property before any vow might be made. So definitely was it understood that tithes belonged to God that to pledge them or divert them or to withhold them was robbery. Thus the divine voice spoke through Malachi to those who had failed to bring their tithes into the storehouse: "Will a man rob God? Yet ye have robbed me. But ye say, Wherein have we robbed thee? In tithes and offerings" (Malachi 3:8).

Tithes, however, could be redeemed. The law was not concerned with the material but with the value. One could substitute a like sum if there was added a fifth to the whole amount paid.

However, there must be absolute honesty in the estimation of values. For example, flocks and herds were tithed by bringing them one by one through a narrow enclosure. As they passed "under the rod" of the owner, every tenth one was regarded as belonging to the Lord. There could be no attempt to select the animals and to substitute as a tithe a poor animal for one which was better. In case of such intended deception both animals were forfeited to the service of the sanctuary, and all possibility of redemption was denied.

Is the law of the tithe *binding on Christians?* Undoubtedly it is, in principle. A certain amount of one's income belongs to the Lord and is to be consecrated to sacred purposes. The injunction of the apostle is quite clear: "Upon the first day of the week let every one of you lay by him his store, as God hath prospered him" (I Corinthians 16:2). Such recognition of the Lord's property must be systematic and proportionate. However, the precise proportion is now left to the conscience of the worshiper.

According to the laws of Leviticus, no person could become very rich or very poor. Under these conditions a fixed fraction of incomes might be reasonable; but, in our present social system, to require a precise proportion of income for religious purposes from all Christians alike might involve a great hardship for some, and relieve others from any real sacrifice or burden. All that should be insisted is that some definite proportion should be adopted, a proportion to change "as the Lord may prosper," and that taking rich and poor together, one-tenth, as an *average minimum*, may be regarded as a proper amount to be devoted to the specific work of the Lord.

The Christian is not bound by exacting rules. He must regard a higher principle, namely, the law of stewardship. All that he has, and not only a definite fraction, belongs to the Lord. If he devotes one-tenth to religious service, he is none the less responsible for the way he employs the remaining nine-tenths. Some day he will be expected to render an account for the use he has made of his Master's goods.

This, however, is no new principle. The ancient tithe, like the first-fruits, recognized that not only the fraction but the whole belonged to the Lord and should be received as a gift and a trust from Him.

Leviticus was written for the instruction of worshipers. Its closing paragraph impressively declares that worship consists not merely in prayer and praise and public ceremonies, but in such complete consecration to God that over person and property alike can be placed this inscription:

Holiness unto the Lord